The Gibraltar Briefcase

The Wise Weapons of Exceptional Executives

Thejendra Sreenivas

Book Publishing Coach

www.thejendra.com

Copyright © 2026 Thejendra Sreenivas

Fourth Edition: 2026

All rights reserved. No part of this publication may be reproduced, distributed, or transmitted in any form or by any means, including photocopying, recording, or other electronic or mechanical methods, without the prior written permission of the author or publisher, except in the case of brief quotations embodied in critical reviews and certain other noncommercial uses permitted by copyright law.

Licensing – If you have purchased an eBook or a digital version of this book, then it's licensed for your personal usage only. It may not be resold or gifted to other people. If you would like to share this with others, please purchase an additional eBook for each person you share it with. If you are reading this and did not purchase it, or it was not purchased for your use only, then please purchase your own copy. Thank you for respecting the publisher's work.

Table of Contents

Preface iii

How to Ask Beautiful Questions 1

When Good People become Bad Bosses 7

Beware of your Super Performers 13

The Folly of First Impressions 19

The Hidden Advantage of Disagreements 27

History -Telescopes to the Future 35

The View from the Hot Seat 43

The Passing of the Crown 49

The Quirky Way to Problem Solving 53

Is Arrogance Creeping in on You? 57

Good Lessons from Bad Bosses 63

Identify Your Stress Triggers 67

When the Hard Way is the Easy Way 77

Unusual Cures for Boring Meetings 83

Top Myths and Facts about Teamwork 93

Workaholics are Not Role Models 99

Why Some People Drive You Nuts 105

Biorhythms – Your Biological Batteries 113

The Power of Reading Management Books 121

Humor – The Ultimate Leadership Style 127

The Dicey Art of Escalation 133

Dealing with Geeks 137

Stop Defining and Typecasting Yourself 141

Get Accustomed to Monotonous Jobs 147

Other Books by the Author 155

    Author Services 159

About the Author 161

Preface

The Gibraltar Briefcase is a bunch of raw advice on management, leadership, and self-improvement for the modern business executive. The Rock of Gibraltar, or Pillar of Hercules, located in Europe, has been standing tough and strong for centuries despite several enemy attacks and long sieges, and nothing can destroy the Rock or its people. The statement *'Solid as the Rock of Gibraltar'* is often used to describe a person who cannot fail or be subdued. To become such a rock, you must continuously repair and detoxify yourself physically, mentally, and spiritually to protect the forts you hold dear. The techniques in this book are the knowledge weapons to help you thrive and survive in modern, stressful workplaces and become like a rock but without turning into a stone.

Ancient humans survived by eating food and fruits in their raw, natural state. But the modern human has become largely dependent on processed, packaged, and contaminated food. Similarly, the modern business executive today has limited access to natural, unadulterated advice and has become accustomed to canned management fodder. This lack of clean advice is leading to constant stress, unrealistic expectations, rapid burnout, etc., for all modern executives worldwide.

Essentially, there are two ways to lead one's life. The first way is you can either slog through life, waste time and energy, or make endless mistakes trying to discover things from your own experience. And the second way is that you can profit from the knowledge and wisdom gained and documented by others. This book shows how you can benefit from the second way. Like a banquet containing an array of delicious, healthy fruits, this book contains a bunch of diverse chapters that can change the way you look at yourself, your colleagues, and the wacky world around you. Though there is no promise of revolutionary magic here, you will definitely see improved results if you use the advice within to guide your future actions. Give it a try. You may be pleasantly surprised.

How to Ask Beautiful Questions

Sometime back, I was watching a TV program on a business channel where a bunch of reputed CEOs, CFOs, COOs, etc., were the judges for a young business entrepreneur program. Each young participant was expected to present a business case for the winning entry. However, the program was going nowhere as the judges weren't allowing any participant to complete their presentation or go beyond a couple of sentences, and they would constantly bombard them with question after question.

The judges were even firing questions at each other and answering every question with another question. Every young participant, half their age, was being ripped to pieces with their incessant and often cynical questions. Finally, one of the participants was awarded a ceramic pot of indeterminate shape with something inscribed on it, while the others walked out dazed and gasping for breath. Mercifully, the program ended soon.

What the above incident teaches you is that the world today is full of people who love to ask tough questions. Interviews, talk shows, blogs, corporate seminars, meetings, vendor discussions, business strategies, IT support, journalism, service level agreements, etc., all love bombarding someone with truckloads of smart and intelligent-sounding questions. Today, asking questions that others cannot answer is a favorite hobby for many people. Hence, many executives nowadays take great pride in asking complicated and smart questions that can make others squirm, shut their mouths, or run away from the scene. Also, many people believe that just asking a tough question settles the matter without the need to get involved to solve the issue. Secondly, a large percentage of people ask tough questions just for the heck of it, especially in meetings.

The basic reason why many people ask tough questions is mainly to satisfy their ego by making others uncomfortable, covering up their lack of knowledge, or just impressing others. For example, most discussions and arguments you may have observed are all about how someone outsmarted someone else by firing a smart question. Watching someone squirm gives a self-congratulatory, sadistic pleasure to many people, like, *'Hah, you should have seen that bozo's face when I asked him that tricky question.'* But it doesn't mean people will be using tough and rude questions with everyone, but they will definitely not miss an opportunity to fire them at someone they can afford to be rude with. Anyway, nowadays, with the amount of information overload, it's very easy to ask plenty of good, bad, tough, smart, rude, tricky, vague, stupid, dumb, and rubbish questions. And a large percentage of those questions just don't have answers.

However, the habit of asking questions is not a bad habit, but deliberately asking questions that you or others cannot answer is dumb. You can keep asking such questions for eternity, but you will not get any correct answers or solutions. Rude and rubbish questions, even smart-sounding ones, often create a lot of problems. Very often, people ask tough questions because they think a tough question will get the necessary answer. But the fact is, people avoid people who ask tough questions. Bombarding anyone with tough questions is a futile exercise because you will never get the right answers. It only makes people avoid you or give you evasive, defensive, and incorrect answers. Besides, a shoot-the-messenger approach will make people tell lies and cover up bad news to prevent their heads from being chewed off. Secondly, rough and tough questions simply create stress, anxiety, and fear in a lot of people. Such questions make people commit more mistakes because the brain goes numb with fear. Toughness prevents the truth from being said, and people will invent excuses. And the list can go on and on. Maybe rough and tough questions are useful in police interrogations, but rarely necessary in business life. As Bob Parsons said, *'Every business everywhere is staffed with imperfect human beings and exists by providing a product or service to other imperfect human beings.'* So, if you are a sensible person, you will understand the limitations of our species.

To get correct answers or solutions from others, you need to ask beautiful questions. Now you may ask what a beautiful question is, and how to ask one? But a beautiful question cannot be exactly defined, nor is it possible to give you a specific list of beautiful questions that can be used in every situation. However, a beautiful question can be described in many ways. Here are a few ways to learn how to ask beautiful questions.

A beautiful question doesn't have any toxicity, cynicism, or tricky content in it. It's a question that does not trap people or put them in an awkward position. A beautiful question can be a straightforward question, but it's asked in a non-threatening or non-intimidating way.

A beautiful question doesn't hurt sentiments, make people defensive, or point fingers at them in an accusatory manner. People make mistakes and will continue to make mistakes in their lifetime. It's quite possible for someone to have completely goofed up on something, lost a major account, or done something really stupid. Except in rare cases, there will always be a valid reason for it.

Beautiful questions create pleasantness and collaboration. They remove fear and extract the right answers, even if the answer is bad news. Successful managers know how to get the right answers from employees by not being intimidating in their approach. Their objective is to solve an issue or a problem, and not get mischievous pleasure by making people uncomfortable. Beautiful questions help you achieve that.

Beautiful questions don't have a 'shoot the messenger' approach. If you develop the habit of asking beautiful questions, then people will approach you openly for help and advice, instead of thinking, 'Here comes the demon to chew our head off.'

People who know how to ask beautiful questions don't thump their fists on tables, demand an explanation immediately, or try to find a scapegoat.

Finally, to summarize, the challenge for each one of us is to frequently pause and observe ourselves to see if we are asking the right questions. And we can conclude this chapter with a quote from Dorothy Nevill, who said, *'The real art of conversation is not only to say the right thing in the right place but to leave unsaid the wrong thing at the tempting moment."*

When Good People become Bad Bosses

As soon as the words 'bad boss' are mentioned, most people start imagining pictures of a wicked person, a crook, a tyrant, a scheming backstabbing individual, a selfish ogre, etc. And the typical textbook definition of a bad boss is the one who screams, threatens, intimidates, grabs credit, fires people, throttles people's necks, and so on. While such gory imaginations could be true in a few cases, it's not so in a large percentage of cases. Actually, it's not necessary to be a wicked person at all to be called a bad boss. Ironically, a good-natured or normal person can also fall into the category of a bad boss without exhibiting any boorish behaviors. To understand how, there are a few common mistakes good people make to slowly transform themselves into bad bosses.

Lack of Knowledge: A good person can become a manager of a department for various reasons, but may have no knowledge necessary to run the department. Often, many employees get promoted to stratospheric levels too fast, but without the required knowledge, maturity, or skills to run a bunch of diverse departments. And this is unavoidable in many cases, as modern managers often have to swim in uncharted waters in today's chaotic business world. However, this can become a catastrophe not only for the manager but also for all his peers and team members who look at him or her for guidance, help, or coaching. If managers lack the required knowledge and advisory skills to coach, mentor, and supervise their department, they can agitate their team members to death.

In addition to stressing their team members daily, managers will also stress themselves more as they will be unable to lead effectively. For example, a good person can be a car service supervisor but can never effectively manage his mechanics if he himself doesn't have some prior experience in servicing a car or at least a generous dose of the practical hardships of it. His lack of knowledge can often lead to conflicts as he may make unrealistic demands on his mechanics, commit to impractical requests by customers, overload his mechanics, etc. Soon, it will become an ego conflict between the *'Knowledgeable and the Clueless.'*

Avoiding Learning: Understandably, a manager cannot be expected to have accurate knowledge from day one. To gain knowledge, one must get into the deep water to understand the nitty-gritty of a new department's work, irrespective of their earlier experience. And no matter which department you manage, there will be some amount of new learning every day to keep abreast of the latest trends and happenings related to that particular industry. But too many managers avoid doing this and don't make any effort to learn the work hands-on, or at least an essential percentage of it. They never bother to understand the 'nuts and bolts' or roll up their sleeves to get involved.

Instead, they run their departments from a high level by viewing the world through status reports, metrics, statistical gymnastics, asking tough questions, etc., and soon become an object of ridicule. Very soon, this will lead to problems like inaccurate estimation, procrastination, inability to make independent decisions, workload issues, staff shortages, endless meetings, email wars, improper budgeting, and various daily conflicts. By refusing to learn or get involved, they distance themselves from understanding any practical issues and difficulties of a department. Instead of being in a position to confidently say, *'Let me show you how'* or *'This is how you do it,'* they will start covering their lack of knowledge through devious means as they become insecure and incompetent. Obviously, that means entering into dirty waters like indulging in cheap politics, surrounding themselves with yes-men, shooting the messenger, and finding scapegoats.

Unable to Shield Their Team: Often, for many managers, maintaining the status of a good and diplomatic person who will not antagonize customers and clients becomes more important than being right. So, they may not be able to shield their team from hostile situations, unfair accusations, or demands. They will start saying yes to every demand and put their team members in trouble or under excessive workloads. Also, they cannot take the heat for their team when required. Very soon, team members will stop going to them for help. As Jeff Rich, the CEO of ACS, says, *'I think the day that your people stop bringing their problems to you is the day you stop* *leading. They've either concluded that you don't care about their problems or that you cannot help them. And leaders have to be in a position to help.'* For example, continuing the example of a mechanic, he will often not be able to shield his mechanics from aggressive and impatient customers who pressurize them with unreasonable demands, invent faults, or expect unrealistic services.

Distorted View: Customers and clients don't appreciate a plain exhibition of good nature. Just because a person is good, customers will not take things easily or dilute their demands. They need value for their money, solutions, answers, guidance, etc., for their problems. And if a person cannot provide that, he or she automatically becomes a bad manager. Good nature and lots of smiles cannot be used as a shield for delivering bad results.

For example, will you go to a doctor who is very friendly but is unable to diagnose your fever or prescribe the right medicines? Will junior surgeons depend on a friendly senior surgeon who cannot teach or oversee complicated and delicate surgeries? Would you go to a lawyer who talks well but gives you bad legal advice? Would you go to or recommend a tax consultant who talks well but can't give you proper tax advice? Similarly, a good-natured person who is unable to help customers, clients, and team members can get into trouble by being branded as a bad manager, as their credibility will take a nosedive.

Finally, we can conclude this chapter with a quote from Thomas Arnold: *'Real knowledge, like everything else of value, is not to be obtained easily. It must be worked for, studied for, thought for, and, more than all, must be prayed for.'*

Beware of your Super Performers

If you have the habit of reading popular business magazines, management books, or articles, you will definitely encounter countless references about various super performers (or hyper-efficient employees) that exist in various organizations, departments, teams, etc. Of course, the definition of a super performer is a subjective term that can vary from manager to manager or from company to company, and can be quite varied based on their personal experiences.

And that picture can range from someone who is super-fast at everything, a noisy person, a flamboyant person, someone who has all the answers, a management's blue-eyed boy, a jargon-emitting person, a go-to person, or even someone who always comes to the office very early and leaves very late, and so on. Or, going by the job advertisements of organizations today, a super performer is someone who meets (or claims to meet) the fancy criteria below (based on real sentences picked from some newspaper advertisements).

1. We are looking for high-value employees dedicated to delivering innovation to assist our clients in high-performance delivery. The employee must be a class of his own and raise his or her sights above the horizon. We are looking for super-efficient leaders who have the challenge to outdo themselves and be a winner all the way.

2. We are looking for a person to lead, motivate, and create a high-performance team capable of continuous innovation and excellence in working for a global leader.

3. We are looking for candidates who are bubbling, energetic, and invigorating to join the sales team of a global winner who can swim in an ocean of opportunities.

Every manager will unquestionably agree that having a gang of such super performers in their teams would be a great thing. However, you may be surprised to know that they can, either quickly or gradually, become your worst nightmare. Over time, and often unknown to you, they can do more harm than good and can slowly curdle or ruin an entire team consisting of normal to good performers. What I am saying may sound ridiculous or stupid, but wait till you hear me out. Some of the top hidden reasons why a super performer can turn a team into a snake pit rather than work as a collaborating team are as below.

While being super-efficient is not a crime, a hyper performer can often make other team members (who work quietly without fanfare) look bad and inefficient, either intentionally or unintentionally. To understand this, just go back to your school and college days. Remember in school where a couple of smart kids would quickly shout answers before the other kids could even understand the teacher's question? They were the class 'know-it-all.' And slowly those speed kids would become the teacher's pets, and the rest of the students would constantly be compared with them, leading to icy jealousy. Similarly, a super performer in a team can corrode the manager's opinion of others, as they will invariably be compared to the team's hero. But people hate being compared with others, as it will make them look inferior and dull. This, in turn, kills teamwork and collaboration and can lead to various internal politics.

Many may argue that having a super performer in a team can be a great source of inspiration for other team members. But the reality is far from this assumption. Constant success is actually a guaranteed way to gain unpopularity. Just like the omnipresent sibling rivalry among kids, a super performer in a team of co-workers will soon be viewed as someone who is hogging all the limelight and the manager's attention or affection, while they are automatically viewed as morons, being unable to do work as efficiently as the super performer. Apart from the usual feelings of envy, it can also lead to fear among coworkers. So, team members will start viewing the super performer as a danger to their survival rather than an inspirational soul.

Managers will intentionally (or unintentionally) start diverting all the juicy jobs to the super performers and the routine/mundane work to others, thereby depriving them of getting ahead or getting involved. Other team members will start feeling they are getting unequal amounts of a manager's attention and responses.

Appreciation can be intoxicating and addictive. Once a peak performer gets continuous attention and appreciation, the natural tendency is to seek activities and tasks that can earn them more and more limelight or rewards. So, they will start invading other team members' territories by finding fault in the way others work, showing off how they could handle the same job better, giving smarter suggestions, etc., thereby making the other team member look stupid. And in many cases, super performers in their desire to remain at the top will start grabbing ideas and pieces of work (or even entire work) from others, thereby depriving others of their rightful share of the workload, or maybe even making them lose their jobs.

Like a child that gets bored with every toy within hours or days and expects its parents to buy a new toy, super performers by nature are restless individuals constantly seeking new activities that will excite them. But a manager or an organization cannot find or invent exciting work perpetually to keep their super performers happy. And because of the halo surrounding them and the holy throne they sit on, they will be unwilling to do ordinary, mundane, and routine work that is essential in any department.

Hence, super performers will refuse, avoid, or quietly offload such activities to their coworkers as they start believing such menial activities are to be done only by the lesser mortals of their team. This can lead to various workload conflicts.

So, as you can see from the above points, you have as much to fear about super performers as you have to fear about inefficient and troublesome workers. And such things could be happening right under your nose, just waiting to explode at the most inconvenient time. However, if you can recognize the smoke signals early to apply the necessary brakes periodically, then you can ensure that everyone in the team can contribute to their strengths and weaknesses without stepping on each other's toes. Finally, at the end of the day, one should understand that super performers can shine and bloom only because bad, normal, and good performers exist around them. And we can conclude this chapter with a quote that says, *'Either super competence or super incompetence may be offensive to an establishment.'*

The Folly of First Impressions

It has often been said that you don't have to commit a great deed for someone to like or hate you. You can be admired or despised for just about anything you do, or don't do. And everyone on our planet has their share of admirers and haters from various people they know or even don't know. But have you wondered why people like or hate somebody, even the ones they have never met before or personally interacted with? The obvious answers could be plenty, but the starting trigger for this judgmental behavior usually lies in one hidden reason. And that hidden reason is the 'first impression' or a 'memory burn' that occurs with the very first encounter we have with someone.

A large percentage of people make their lasting impressions and judgments about others within the first few minutes of an encounter. The encounter can be in the form of a meeting, reading, hearing, or just seeing something (positive or negative) about them. In many cases, people can form pleasant to completely warped opinions of someone just by looking at a photograph of a person whom they may not even know personally. First impressions are so powerful that their effects can often last a lifetime and will influence all future mutual interactions. While this could be a popular method of framing judgments by millions of people, blindly following such a method can often do more harm than good. Though many people swear by first impressions, on close examination, they are often wrong and misleading in most cases. For example, to see how easily we can be influenced by what we read about someone, let us use a small joke that I had read somewhere. The slightly modified joke is as follows.

Suppose it's time to elect a new world leader, and you have to decide to select him or her. But you have to make a selection based only on the candidate's description without knowing who exactly they are, while their real names are inside a sealed envelope. Now, who would you vote for?

Candidate-A: Associates with crooked politicians and consults with astrologists. He's had two mistresses, chain smokes, and drinks 8 to 10 martinis a day.

Candidate-B: He was kicked out of office twice, sleeps until noon, arrogant type, used opium in college, and drinks a quart of whiskey every evening.

Candidate-C: He is a decorated war hero. He is mostly a vegetarian, always smiling, loves his own people, doesn't smoke, drinks an occasional beer, and has never cheated on his wife.

Which of these candidates would be your choice? It will most probably be Candidate-C.

Now open the envelopes and read out the names.

Candidate A is Franklin D. Roosevelt

Candidate B is Winston Churchill

Candidate C is Adolf Hitler

The above example will show how you can be easily fooled by what you read and easily frame opinions about someone if you don't dig further. This is how people normally get misled by first impressions. We quickly frame opinions and judgments of others without even meeting them based on what we hear, read, or see about them from various sources. It happens to each one of us many times in our lifetime. So, if you had all along believed that first impressions were useful or guaranteed judgment methods, here are a few reasons why you should never solely depend on them.

On our planet, a very large percentage of people give too much importance to first impressions to form their permanent perceptions about someone. But it's wrong to brand a person permanently based on what you saw or heard for a brief time. Maybe you caught the person at the wrong time or wrong place. Maybe you were not getting the complete picture or facts. Being in the wrong place at the wrong time is not a crime or always avoidable. Everybody cannot be in the right place at the right time or say the right things at the right moment to make a stunning first impression. The same rules apply to you too. Hence, people need several impressions both ways to know and understand each other. It takes a long time to understand someone and cannot be based on a singular or brief incident.

Appearances can be deceptive. It has been said that people look normal until you get to know them better. The reverse is also true. People can also look abnormal until you get to know them better. Hence, you should always aim to know people leisurely, and you will soon discover they just have faults different from yours. And history is full of numerous cases of people who have made awesome first impressions but failed miserably later. For example, a well-dressed and smooth-talking person displaying a great first impression may eventually turn out to be a con man, while a mediocre person with an initial shabby personality may prove to be an honest, trustworthy person.

To quote another example, when we first met our college biology professor, most students were taken aback by his small, meek structure and somewhat odd behavior. But when he started his lectures on botany, he was awesome. His lectures were so electrifying, and he could hold the entire class in a hypnotic trance through his powerful teaching and great anecdotes. Though a lot of students were aiming for engineering, nobody would miss his class, and not a single cranky student would disturb his session.

First impressions should not be confused with intuition, which is entirely different. Intuition is a mysterious message we get that can give us a warning about someone. The first impression I am referring to is mainly about real-world stuff like physical appearance, dress, handwriting, mediocrity, shyness, weak or strong handshakes, color, speech abilities or disabilities, nervousness, etiquette issues, ignorant and unintentional acts, cultural behaviors, etc. Don't judge a book by its cover. Lack of flamboyance is not a lack of capability, as believed by Mary Kay Ash, the legendary founder of Mary Kay Cosmetics, a billion-dollar cosmetics giant. It has often been observed that she never paid much attention to anyone's physical appearance and always focused on who he or she was as a person. Positive dressing and impressive displays, though necessary in the business world, can never be a substitute for getting things done and achieving results.

As a reputed manager once said, *'Give me a team in denims and T-shirts who can do the job efficiently, caring for the customers and who are real and secure about themselves, rather than people with very little substance.'* Often, people who spend too much time dressing and behaving elegantly to make great first impressions are usually hollow, as they spend too much time in front of the mirror and too little time growing their knowledge, products, and people.

The Folly of First Impressions

Many people proudly claim they have the magic or psychic ability to easily judge a person just with one glance or a brief encounter. But such a claim is completely naïve and misleading. Only ignorant or gullible people take first impressions as permanent characteristics. Except in some hard-core cases, the person you may have seen last year is not necessarily the same person next year, as human beings are dynamic creatures and constantly changing (or evolving) for better or worse. But true professionals, leaders, and credible establishments like the law courts in most developed and democratic countries never get influenced or carried away by first impressions.

They always believe in a thorough investigation, facts, proof, etc., no matter how tedious or long it takes. They always make their independent assessments about someone based on facts. Otherwise, if first impressions were assumed to be correct and let loose, then thousands of people would be hanged, lynched, and buried alive based on media hype, overwhelming public opinion, and trial by media, newspaper reports, etc.

However, with all the above arguments against first impressions, there are certain areas and a percentage of cases where judgments based on first impressions are true and correct. On our planet, nothing is 100% right or wrong. So, for example, while dealing with street punks, people who are a menace to society, the stubbornly obnoxious, criminally oriented, and those who deliberately exhibit boorish behaviors, etc., you can easily take your first impressions as final without bothering to investigate further. But you must consciously remember that such cases will normally be applied only to a small percentage of cases, and any negative experiences based on such encounters must not be universally applied to the remaining large percentage of cases.

Finally, we can conclude this chapter with a great quote from Violet Asquith, a British politician, who said, *'The first time you see Winston Churchill, you see all his faults, and the rest of your life you spend discovering his virtues."*

The Hidden Advantage of Disagreements

A popular comic strip once showed a soldier diligently watering a lawn in the rain. When a puzzled passerby questions the need for a hose during rain, the soldier answers that he was simply following orders that the lawn must be watered every day. And then mischievously adds that soldiers are forbidden from disagreeing or questioning the orders made by their superiors.

Conventional wisdom usually shows that going quietly with the established flow is the path to success and happiness. For example, if you are the boss and you have team members who don't support you in everything, you may argue that it can undermine morale, reduce your authority, weaken the team, or project or even sabotage the company's goals. So, a good team player is the one who does not rock the boat, delay decisions, or introduce roadblocks. And obviously, having people who agree with you on anything and everything has many perceived advantages, like below.

1. Working with cooperative people is a joy and necessary to achieve a goal. After all, who would like to work with people who disagree?

2. Things get done faster when you have people who agree with you on anything and everything.

3. With people who collaborate easily, there will be fewer conflicts, stress, and irritation.

And so on. The above reasons appear valid because people see disagreements in the workplace lead to anger, confusion, fear, embarrassment, etc., and so it must be avoided at all costs. However, putting the popular reasons aside for some time, there are several hidden reasons why surrounding yourself with yes-men, apple-polishers, and people who blindly agree without questioning for various reasons (including fear) can actually be a poison pill for you. While preventing disagreements may have valid reasons in the armed forces, the same formula in the civilian and corporate world can often become a disaster, as you will soon see.

To be truly successful, you must periodically welcome a generous dose of disagreement in every major or important decision you take, even if you are an expert in what you do. The suggestion for openly inviting disagreement may seem odd because it can be infuriating, insulting, irritating, and seen as a roadblock to your plans. But beneath the hood, there are several advantages of accepting people who can question your plans, decisions, demands, ideas, etc., provided you learn the ability to see it objectively. Many times, the advantages of seeking advice from people who dare to disagree can often far outweigh the advantages of surrounding yourself with only those who agree. The reasons why you need some disagreements are as follows.

Lack of dissent and disagreement means a lack of analysis. Everything has a downside when viewed from certain angles. This has been aptly demonstrated by Alfred Sloan (CEO of General Motors from 1923 to 1956), who once said in a directors' meeting, *'Gentlemen, I take it that we are all in complete agreement on the decision here. Then, I propose that we postpone further discussion to give ourselves time to develop disagreement and perhaps gain some understanding of what the decision is all about.*' If Alfred Sloan couldn't find opposition to an important decision, he would postpone it to give his business managers some time to think about the pros and cons in different ways.

A disagreement can often prevent you from rushing into bad decisions and choices. They give you time and press the brakes to ponder over it, though you may get irritated by the delay and roadblocks. You may have done extensive homework on a decision but still may have overlooked a simple but important point, which the dissenting person can see when looked at from a different angle.

Use disagreements to your advantage. Cynics, pessimists, and people who disagree are right nine times out of ten. Hence, learn how to extract gold from it. When you are doing a project or a major task, you need people who can blurt out problems and roadblocks openly, not someone who will gleefully say everything can be done and pat your back. Every time a cynic opens his mouth, you know what exactly needs to be fixed so that a project can succeed. Ask yourself, 'How can I use this information?' or 'How much time, money, and effort is involved to solve all these problems?'

You need to accept opposition objectively and professionally. You should encourage people to disagree with you so that all sides of the decision can be carefully examined. Unless you are a megalomaniac or an extremely dismissive person, you must accept the fact that countless people below or above you will be more talented, smarter, knowledgeable, and more powerful than you. It's not enough to invite dissent and criticism because it's the new management fad or just for the heck of it, and later victimize or target the person for saying something you didn't like to hear.

Don't be afraid to disagree or accept disagreement. Real leaders accept disagreement. Surrounding yourself with yes-men simply means they are just rubber-stamping everything you say without adding any value or digging deep into the issue. A certain amount of honest friction heightens interest and establishes mutual respect. However, when dealing with subordinates, you have to invite dissent by asking beautiful questions. People beneath you will never openly dissent if you have blown your fuse or acted irrationally earlier. Many employees, especially newcomers, will not speak up in an atmosphere where they feel their ideas are not welcome.

If you are famous or popular, everyone around you will always agree with you and applaud all your decisions. If you notice such a thing, then you need to be extra careful of those who are too supportive of your ideas and suggestions. This is because they will also not prevent you from making mega mistakes. So, whether you decide to buy unsuitable equipment for your organization or even go to the extent of cooking the books to commit some fraud, they will not oppose or openly dissent. Later on, when something goes badly wrong, the yes-men around will quickly disappear and not share the blame by promptly claiming that it was all your decision. Of course, if they had disagreed earlier, but you did not care or bulldozed their opinions, then only you are to be solely blamed.

Another key to managing disagreements is to prevent them from taking a personal turn, as 99% of disagreements turn into conflicts and become dirty. The simple reason for this is the way a disagreement is put forth. Many a time, a particular suggestion or idea may invoke a swift and brutal objection due to various reasons, bad past experiences, or the way it's proposed. A disagreement has to be strongly focused on the issue or idea, and not on the person or the way the person blurted out the opinion, body language, bad choice of words, etc. Though etiquette counts, the emotional aspect must be carefully and consciously filtered out so that you can refocus on the issue or, in extreme cases, abandon the idea completely.

One must also understand that disagreement and dissent should not be done just for the sake of it, like opposition politicians who have a standard policy to oppose everything that the ruling party does. Arguing just for the sake of arguing is also not productive disagreement.

Finally, we can conclude this chapter with two great quotes on agreeing.

'The fellow that agrees with everything you say is either a fool or he is getting ready to skin you."- Kin Hubbard

'The people to fear are not those who disagree with you, but those who disagree with you and are too cowardly to let you know." - Napoleon Bonaparte

History -Telescopes to the Future

Nowadays, if you read interviews of any top business people in any news media, you will invariably see a question that asks which book they have recently read or are currently reading. And their obvious answers will be the names of some newfangled management book like *Why the Moon Is Still Round While the Earth Is Going Flat*, or *The Fifteenth Leadership Habit of a Maverick*, or some new cutting-edge book about managing people, or even some fancy novel. But you will never hear any businessman say they are reading an ordinary book like a medieval or ancient history textbook.

Now, you may argue how a boring textbook on history helps a businessperson run his or her business. Besides, who has the time to read history, and who cares if some Attila the Hun plundered a village in the fourth century or some king was beheaded by his courtiers? And why bother with what has been over and forgotten, and what is the justification to study something unconnected with modern business issues?

After all, every modern guru preaches the need to look into the future and not look at the past. Common convincing arguments, but you may be surprised to know that reading and understanding history actually have immense business benefits. Hidden inside history lies an immense wealth of advice and real case studies that can not only help every businessman but practically everyone, whether connected with a business or not. But a history book will not help any businessman if read in the traditional way of simply memorizing events, dates, names, etc., intended to just pass an exam. To extract business gold from history, you need to read it from a completely different angle. And that angle is to concentrate on what mistakes our forefathers made and how you can avoid them. If you had thought that history was just a boring school subject that must be tolerated only until you pass that dreadful exam, just look at the points in its favor below.

There is a common saying that history repeats itself. This is proved by the fact that one of the biggest mistakes people make is constantly repeating the mistakes that others made. And people suffer because they ignore and avoid history. People easily fall into the same black holes that others fell into a short while ago. Or they confidently predict the future while experimenting with a sugar-coated plan that our forefathers burnt their hands with. This is because people are unable or unwilling to read the warning signs of history, readily visible all over the place. However, if you ignore or avoid history, you end up repeating the exact mistakes your forefathers or predecessors made, along with almost identical and disastrous results. But if you read history, it can give you hundreds of years of great wisdom and examples to learn from, especially what to avoid rather than what to experiment with and repeat.

Abraham Lincoln once said, *'Human action can be modified to some extent, but human nature cannot be changed.'* This has proved to be true for centuries and will prove to be true forever. Except in obvious areas like technology, medicine, scientific research, etc., there is nothing new under the sun when it comes to managing people. But most businessmen and B-school gurus think they have discovered a revolutionary new management concept fresh out of the oven on how people can be managed. Unfortunately, they do not realize that a similar or identical one would have been experimented with elsewhere because they did not bother to read history. The human behavioral patterns of what is going on right now would have definitely occurred somewhere in the past.

History is not really some useless stuff, as most people think. History prevents you from reinventing the wheel. Albert Einstein once said, '*Insanity is doing the same thing over and over again and expecting different results.*' Throughout history, people have committed the same mistakes of trying to subdue people, wage wars, commit treachery, and various forms of atrocities on each other, leading to the same guaranteed disastrous results as experienced earlier.

Modern man is no different, and even today, you see dictators and cruel people ruling many countries and organizations. And similar crimes and follies occur inside workplaces with equivalent disastrous results. Hence, it's highly necessary to read history as it teaches the current generation to understand things that don't work or never worked in the past. If you can understand history from the right perspective, it can help the present business managers and executives to avoid needless and futile experimentation with people management. By learning the patterns of events in history, you can recognize the repetition of the same patterns in what is going on around you today.

History will not tell you where you are going, but it will tell you how you got there. What you did in the past decided the present, and what you do now will later decide the future. History offers a wealth of information about how people, societies, and even civilizations behave. History can teach you some great lessons in people management, like the mistakes our ancestors made, the disastrous consequences, the fall from grace of mighty leaders and dictators, and many great ups and downs.

History is splattered with examples of bad people management and its disastrous results. Many kings have been assassinated due to their poor people management by the very people they trusted. For example, Julius Caesar was stabbed by his trusted friend Brutus. Many have been beheaded for their follies. Wars have started due to abuse, criticism, and harassment. Applied to business organizations, people make the same mistakes again and again, but disguise them as newer or modern management theories and learning experiences. But by reading and understanding history, you can avoid repeating the same mistakes again and again. History helps you look at both the past and future at once. And you can constantly educate yourself from those who were born earlier than you and become like Janus, the Roman god who had two heads back-to-back to look into the future and the past at the same time.

History helps create good businesspeople and professionals, though it may not exactly define a specific job profile in the corporate world. But studying the global past gives one the knowledge and flexibility required in many work situations. For example, you can develop good research skills and use historical examples to design modern business plans. The wisdom of Aristotle or Socrates told centuries ago is still valid for many business successes and failures. Knowledge of history is an asset for a variety of work and professional situations in the modern global context. History helps in identifying, understanding, and avoiding cultural sensitivities. It provides evidence about how nations have interacted with other countries and societies in the past, and how that long-standing enmity or friendship between the countries can affect business.

Finally, we can conclude this chapter with a great quote on history from Winston Churchill: *'The farther backward you can look, the farther forward you are likely to see."*

The View from the Hot Seat

Violet Asquith, a British politician, once said, *'The first time you see Winston Churchill, you see all his faults, and the rest of your life you spend discovering his virtues."* The essence of this statement can also be reversed: 'The first time you see someone you may see all their virtues, and then slowly you will see their faults and failures.' Many a time we get into situations where we strongly believe a particular person may be the right candidate for a position, job, or even to be the ruler of a nation based on their great ideas or the vibrant energy they seem to emit.

But after they enter into that responsible position where their ideas and energy seemed so perfectly fit, they will somehow miserably fail, and none of their ideas work. They appear to walk in as saviors but walk out as failures. Or in some cases, you may believe you can easily handle a particular task due to your experience or subject knowledge but get stonewalled and fail. For example, we see numerous examples of flashy sports coaches failing, a business manager highly successful in one firm failing miserably elsewhere, a politician failing big time as a minister, and so on.

So, why is it that people who promise the moon and claim to revolutionize the system fail miserably when they actually get the baton? Why do good ideas often not work, and why does knowledge or confidence fail? While there could be several straightforward reasons why ordinary people fail, the hidden (and even philosophical) reasons why confident people and experts fall down is because they fail to understand that self-confidence and assumptions are very different from ground realities. To understand what I am talking about, you need to absorb a concept called - *view from the hot seat*. Let me elaborate on this with a couple of examples.

Dionysius was a fourth-century B.C. tyrant of Syracuse in ancient Greece. Once he overheard a young man named Damocles envying his good fortune and blabbering about how easily he could also rule the nation if he had all the power and resources at his disposal. So, Dionysius decided to teach Damocles a lesson by making him ruler for a day. The excited Damocles was made a king for a day and treated to all the royal ceremonies. As Damocles sat feasting in the palace, he happened to glance upward and was horrified to see a sharp sword hanging above his head using just a thin horsehair. This scared the hell out of Damocles. Dionysius then explained what that sword symbolized by saying, '*I have many enemies. As I have come to power by violence, my life is always in danger and anything can happen to me at any time. Every day that I rule this city, my life is in as much danger as yours is at this moment.*' It was then that Damocles understood the job of a ruler is not as easy as he had imagined. The harsh reality and an overwhelming sense of a king's responsibilities became clear only when Damocles sat on the throne (hot seat), but had no clue about it previously. Basically, the king was telling Damocles, '*Just sit in my hot seat and feel its temperature.*'

Let us take another example of your first time driving a car, bicycle, or motorbike. Until then you would have most probably believed driving was an easy and effortless affair. But as soon as you sat in the driver's seat for the first time in your life, the view of the traffic world would have definitely scared you. Or even if you knew driving, it can be scary if you now have to drive in a high-paced, reckless city. This vaporizing of confidence, seeing the big picture, or realizing the gravity of the situation is what is known as the *view from the hot seat*.

Here are a few things one should know about this concept. The hot seat view can be a valuable lesson for everyone, as it teaches you the real reasons for success or failure in anything you or others do. It is only when you sit in the hot seat you can see things that others can't see. For example, voters and journalists may easily criticize a politician for not fulfilling his election promises. But the politician now sitting in the hot seat will see compulsions, political pressures, unspeakable issues, skeletons in the cupboard, hidden dangers, stonewalls, etc., that limit what he can or cannot do. This is why people in power are often unable to solve a problem or fix a mess that they would have earlier confidently promised or claimed to do.

A popular saying says it's not necessary to be truly knowledgeable about something to argue about it. We are all guilty of preaching great advice, and everyone thinks they can do it until they have to actually do it. This is why our planet is full of armchair commandos (you and I included) who can easily give top advice on

The View from the Hot Seat

how an airline hijack could have been handled, improve the economy, run a government, fight a war, handle terrorism, win a game, and so on. But it's not that easy, as spectators will often not have the full picture of a situation until they are inside and get a grip on the hurdles of the job.

Everyone can do somebody's job in their imagination. But it's not easy to be in a position where you are responsible for important or difficult decisions. Similarly, flamboyant talking is different from doing. For example, people who engage in such talk often sound confident and articulate. They can easily spray facts and opinions and have interesting ideas. However, except in some rare cases, it's always wrong to believe such talkative people are also good implementers. For example, if you make them sit on the hot seat, you will see they will often be no different from others.

There is also a philosophical angle to this. Sometimes you may know what to do, how to do it, and have all the apparent powers, yet you will be unable to complete a task due to seemingly unrelated factors. This is when you need to believe in the mischievous hand of fate. Believe in the possibility that many things are probably not destined to be done by you. There is many a slip between the cup and the lip. Don't be sure that your plans will work however well and meticulously planned. Destiny works in inexplicable ways. Many times in life you will be so close to winning something, so close to a victory, so close to completing something, etc. But you lose it by a whisker. This old-fashioned expression means don't be too sure that your plan is going to work because anything can go wrong at any time. Between the time you decide to do something and the time you actually do it, things can often go wrong.

Finally, we can conclude this chapter with two beautiful quotes.

'The problem with the world is knowledgeable people are full of self-doubts, while ignorant people are full of self-confidence."

"It is far easier to whisper advice from behind the scenes rather than risk its merit at the point of attack." - from the movie King Ralph

The Passing of the Crown

A general dictionary defines a superpower as, '*An extremely powerful nation, countries capable of influencing international events, global policies, etc., influence acts and policies of less powerful nations, etc.*' For example, if you type the word 'superpower' in any internet search engine it will usually throw up names and articles of countries like the USA, Russia, Japan, China, etc., and their influence in world affairs. And if you read a little bit of history, you can see names of other countries like Egypt, Persia, Greece, Rome, etc., who were all superpowers long, long ago.

On a smaller scale, we also see countless examples of super companies and super individuals who have now either wound up, disintegrated, or simply disappeared without a trace. After reading such stuff it's natural for anyone to wonder how they could not sustain their success despite having all the powers and knowledge to do so. For this, the pundits may give a series of explanations and reasons for the decline. For example, Rome was a superpower in ancient times, had an army with the best training, the best budgets, the finest buildings, etc. But today that empire is nowhere, and any history professor can explain how the Roman Empire disintegrated because a certain emperor did a bunch of silly mistakes. Or, coming to the 21st century, current-day pundits may give a detailed list of a modern country's leadership failures resulting in its decline. Secondly, with the advent of modern media today, there is no dearth of soothsayers who confidently predict who will be the next superpower, super company, or super-individual in the future. But whether such predictions will become true, only time will tell. However, despite truckloads of information available on how a nation, organization, or individual can ascend or descend, there are a few mysterious secrets about success that one should be constantly aware of as described below.

Success is a traveler. The goddess of wealth and fame travels from hand to hand. History is full of examples of such riches-to-rags stories of countries, organizations, and individuals. Logic and rationalism may somehow explain how such downslides happen in our universe, but they cannot explain why they happen. The why reason lies in the naughty way success works. Success is a fickle creature, like a monkey on a tree or a butterfly that jumps from one flower to another. It does not stay in one place. Though it's a natural desire for countries, companies, and people to continuously remain on the top, Mother Nature does not allow that. It will ensure they fail and decline after some time, and will never allow a single entity to hog the limelight forever. Hence, nobody can remain at the top perpetually, no matter how smart they are or how hard they try.

When great nations, organizations, or individuals decline you may ask, why on earth do such bad things happen and how did they fail despite following the so-called best practices that made them climb to superpower status? For this, people may say it's because the universe is a random, chaotic dance of meaningless happenings. This may seem true because we see several personal and singular 'riches-to-rags' stories that just don't make sense. But, on an overall scale, underneath all the chaotic occurrences there are hidden reasons and purposes for many things that happen around. Call it fate, destiny, or luck, but accept the fact that the baton will change hands, and the emperor's crown will get a new head to sit on temporarily. So, learn to tune into the mysterious way our nature works.

Success has no loyalty and can ditch anyone at any time. It can go from anyone to anyone and is always unpredictable. Also, success is not too choosy or logical about the competency or worthiness of the person it's gifting itself to. That is, if Person-A is currently a good capable person, and suppose success decides to ditch him, it will not necessarily choose another good capable person to cling to. Just look around and you can see countless such examples of things going from good to bad, and bad to worse.

Success is restless and gets bored easily. It's not faithful to anyone. Even if one is doing all the apparent right things it's not possible to retain or sustain success. Like a child that gets bored of every toy within hours or days and expects its parents to buy a new toy, success by nature is a restless individual constantly seeking new owners to latch on to.

Finally, we can conclude this chapter with a quote that says, *'When humans are too happy, even the gods are jealous.' - Old jungle saying.*

The Quirky Way to Problem Solving

Among all the creatures on our planet, only we humans have the remarkable ability to solve (and also create) various problems. But many a time, we cannot resolve problems and issues that trouble us, no matter how hard we try to use conventional methods. And those conventional methods we normally use are to either constantly brood over it, debate it to eternity, or collect truckloads of data in the hope that it will help us arrive at a solution. However, despite such intense efforts, the solutions will often evade us.

To understand why, one should note that problem-solving is a mysterious science that sometimes goes beyond conventional thinking, objective analysis, left-brain rationality, etc. In order to solve many pressing problems that haunt us, one should occasionally ignore the conventional methods and instead enter the world of unconventional thinking. Many a time, unconventional methods can easily solve problems that conventional methods cannot. Given below are a few such methods that one can try when stuck with a nagging problem.

Let it go: We often believe a solution will appear if we keep attacking a problem relentlessly. Unfortunately, that is not the right way, as solving many problems is similar to chasing a beautiful butterfly. The harder you try to catch it, the farther it flies away. But, surprisingly, if you stand still, that butterfly will start flying very close to you or may even sit on your shoulder. Similarly, as a popular quote tells, *'If you want something very badly, first set it free,'* you may have to first let go of a nagging problem for some time. Forcefully eject it from your mind and give it some time to clear the mental fog. When you do that, suddenly you can discover new ways and obvious solutions dropping in that can seem vastly superior to your previous thoughts. This is the paradox of letting go, where the solution pops up only when you let go and give up instead of clinging on desperately.

Sleep over it: Each one of us is a mysterious and magnificent machine. Behind our normal physical existence, there lies a vast untapped world that we are not fully aware of. There are countless incredible skills and powers that we have, but never know or don't know how they work. Even today one never knows why solutions evade us when we are vigorously trying to solve, but pop in mysteriously when we least expect it or when we are asleep. In many cases, it's intuition and dreams that give us an answer to a problem that is impossible to get when we are awake. For example, one of the most revolutionary findings in organic chemistry was the discovery of the structure of the benzene molecule. The scientist Friedrich Kekule worked for years to discover its atomic structure without success. But one night, he dreamt of many snakes circling together and forming a ring of six snakes chasing each other's tails. When he awoke, he got the answer, which was the shape hexagon as the elusive structure of the benzene ring.

Wait for the destined hour: Sometimes you have to think philosophically. Many a time you may think, *'Why was I racking my brain when the solution was so simple, or why couldn't I think of it before?'* But, as Ovid, a Roman poet, once said, 'Everything comes gradually at its appointed hour.' Similarly, many solutions arrive only at the appointed hour and not before, no matter how hard you try.

Finally, we can conclude this chapter with a great quote from Albert Einstein, who said, *'The intellect has little to do on the road to discovery. There comes a leap in consciousness, call it intuition or what you will, and the solution comes to you, and you don't know how or why."*

Is Arrogance Creeping in on You?

A general dictionary defines arrogance in many ways: '*Offensive display of superiority, self-importance, overbearing pride, pompous, haughtiness, behaving in a superior manner toward inferiors, etc.*' Each one of us would have definitely seen or experienced arrogance by someone at some time. An arrogant person can impact you in many ways, and depending on your current position you may or may not be able to control such people.

For example, an arrogant professor, teacher, boss, or reputed personality can make life hell for all his subordinates and continue to behave with brazen superiority to everyone for years. Often, you will not be able to do anything because such people control your core necessities like passing exams, promotions, salary hikes, sales figures, brand, etc. But in some cases, you can hit back with all your power at arrogant people. Nevertheless, arrogant people in all walks of life are a pain and will be an important topic of discussion everywhere. Behind-the-back gossip like,

'He or she has become arrogant now, but wasn't like that before,' is quite common in most workplaces, amongst friends, relatives, etc. However, it doesn't mean arrogant people will be boorish with everyone, but they will definitely not miss an opportunity to demonstrate it to someone they can afford to be rude with.

Often, the person being branded arrogant may not truly realize they have indeed become arrogant. For example, we rarely think of ourselves as being arrogant, as we usually believe it's always someone else who can be arrogant, but not us. But arrogance does exist to various degrees in everyone, including you and me. Now suppose you discover that people who matter to you are calling you arrogant behind your back? Or worse, someone tells you flat on your face that you are indeed arrogant.

What will be your reaction? It can rudely jolt you from the grand benevolent image you hold of yourself. Being branded arrogant is something that nobody would like to hear. You could get furious, outraged, and vehemently disagree with their opinion. Or, if you can control your senses, you can stop and think of it as a wake-up call to mend your ways.

Arrogance is like a special body odor that you can't smell, but others can. But unless somebody tells you openly, or you have a mirror of Snow White's stepmother, you don't get to realize it. Similar to how people recognize the harmful effects of junk food, high cholesterol, etc., it's also important to recognize some vital signs that could make one arrogant over time. So, what are those signs that can make you arrogant? Here are seven signs that could make you arrogant over time unless you take appropriate steps to puncture your bloated ego periodically.

Knowledge: Your subject knowledge is good and improving day by day. People come to you for advice, tips, and guidance. You have all the answers for anything and everything, or you believe so. Soon, you begin to think you have become an expert in everything and feel others are now dependent on you. And you gradually become dismissive of suggestions and recommendations by others, except yours, of course.

Salary: You have a juicy salary. You can pay all your bills, loans, and expenses and still have plenty of spare money to buy the things you desire. Your bank balance makes you feel invincible, and you start comparing everyone based on the money they make.

Job title: You have a fancy job title that can create an aura of awe around you. Titles having groovy words like global, enterprise, strategy, leader, etc., can quietly corrupt a person's ego faster than a person who has a mediocre title like sales manager, though both could be doing identical ordinary jobs.

Contacts: You develop contacts and connections with reputed people, famous personalities, top brass, etc., and hover around important people. You have the blessings of a powerful godfather who worships the ground you walk on, protects you, listens to you, and does not make a move without consulting you. So, you now feel like a VIP with the power to crush ordinary mortals.

Successes: Frequent success and winning can be a powerful arrogance booster. For example, you have had a series of successes and promotions that are the envy of others. Everything you touch turns to gold. Or you have been very smart and quick in burying your failures before anyone notices them. Or somebody is doing the work and producing the results, while you are getting the rewards and hikes. During temporary lucky periods in life, a feeling of Midas touch can get into people's heads. This is often the reason why many sportspersons, film personalities, business owners, etc., become haughty and pushy.

Answers: You don't provide solutions to questions anymore. Instead, you now answer every question with another smart question. You develop the skill to invent a dozen jargon-filled smart, tough, and tricky questions on the fly that can make others squirm, chew their head off, or make them flee from the scene. Of course, you don't need to know the answers, or if answering is unavoidable, you can invent some more jargon-filled questions to confuse the other party.

Personal: In addition to the above factors, an individual's personal qualities, or Mother Nature's temporary gifts to humans like young age, physical strength, beauty, good health, IQ, etc., can also make one arrogant.

Finally, the challenge for each one of us is to frequently pause and observe ourselves to see if any of the above factors are making us pompous. And we can conclude with a quote from Henry W. Shaw: *'It is not only the most difficult thing to know oneself but the most inconvenient one, too.'*

Good Lessons from Bad Bosses

Today, among the myriads of workplace troubles, having a bad boss is probably the worst that can happen to an employee. And the typical textbook definition of a bad boss is the one who screams, threatens, intimidates, disrespects, grabs credit, fires people, throttles people's necks, and so on. Bad bosses exist in all organizations, though the definition of a bad boss (or a bad employee) is a vague and subjective term that can be debated for eternity depending on whose side you lean on an issue. In fact, the more competitive the organization, the more you see and hear stories about such people.

Nobody likes working for a bad boss, and most would gladly jump ship at the first chance to escape, even if they are passionate about their work. Long ago, a classmate of mine quit an extremely reputed scientific institute, unable to work for a toxic chemistry professor, though he was ready to sacrifice an arm and a leg for chemistry. Nevertheless, apart from a generous dose of ulcers, gloominess, and some hair loss due to a bad boss, there are ways to turn this situation to your advantage. However, most people are normally unaware of how they can actually gain valuable lessons from the idiosyncrasies of a bad boss. But it's quite easy if you learn to look at it peculiarly. Instead of craving a pleasant workplace every day, just think unconventional and start imagining it as a training institute to learn some exciting lessons in behavioral psychology. So, until you can escape to a better workplace or until the bad boss self-destructs, you can continuously imbibe several valuable lessons. A few lessons are mentioned below.

A bad boss can be a walking textbook on behavioral psychology. Working with a bad boss is your golden chance to learn the do's and don'ts of management. In all probability, you can learn more about people management working with a bad boss in six months than working with a good boss for five years.

Bad bosses help you learn the harsh realities of human nature and make you better prepared for life's countless encounters. You swim better when you learn to swim in a rough river or sea, rather than in a calm swimming pool.

Every growl, rude remark, goof-up, threat, cover-up, charm switching, etc., can be a good lesson that is going to pay rich dividends to you at a later stage. They help you become a better manager at a later stage because you will now have a rich experience in the pitfalls of bad management. It helps you to instantly remember and avoid the wrong things when faced with similar or equivalent situations. For example, it may help you remember that it's not a good idea to throw a paperweight at an employee who is a member of the local trade union. :-)

And bad bosses help you in many other ways if you study their lives carefully. For example, it will help you understand how and why many employees erupt like a volcano at home due to work-related problems.

Worldwide, many ordinary people have become great leaders because they were subject to various degrees of insults or extreme forms of harassment by someone. So, directly or indirectly, every great leader will have to thank their tormentors for their current greatness. Similarly, it can also perhaps make you great someday.

So, you now see having a bad boss is not really such a bad thing after all. And we can conclude this chapter with a great Chinese proverb that says, '*A gem cannot be polished without friction, nor man perfected without trials.*'

Identify Your Stress Triggers

If you type the word 'stress' in any internet search engine, you will get a billion pieces of information related to stress and the harm it can cause. A general dictionary defines stress as, '*A specific response by the body to a stimulus, as fear or pain that disturbs or interferes with the normal physiological equilibrium of an organism, mental, or emotional strain or tension.*' The word stress is derived from the Latin word 'stringere,' meaning to 'draw tight,' describing hardships.

Every day, millions of people around the world experience stress ranging from mild dosages to extreme cases that lead to several complicated health disorders. Even animals, insects, and plants experience various degrees of stress due to several reasons. Dr. Hans Selye, a reputed author of numerous papers and books on stress, says headaches, insomnia, high blood pressure, and heart and kidney diseases are the common problems created by stress. According to his expert opinion, 'Every stress leaves an indelible scar, and the organism pays for its survival after a stressful situation by becoming a little older.' When you are stressed, your adrenal glands produce a hormone called cortisol. Cortisol is a highly toxic substance that attacks muscles and organs and rapidly diminishes your strength. It also diminishes your immune system, leading to various kinds of mental and physical disorders. Stress is your body's natural response to everyday physical, emotional, and environmental demands.

Many people often confuse stress with plain tiredness. Whenever you ask someone if they are stressed, they immediately say they are okay or feeling fine. But the reality is different. You could be highly stressed but not physically tired. This is because stress is a silent killer and creeps into a person silently. You cannot avoid stress totally in today's life, especially in today's modern, complex workplace. It is a mental thing that has the potential to create complicated health disorders. To understand the difference between stress and tiredness, just imagine a hot cup of soup. The hot soup can contain very little salt or a high quantity of salt. The quantity of salt (saltiness) is comparable to stress, while the temperature (hotness) is comparable to tiredness. The saltiness of the soup does not reduce even when it cools down. Similarly, a person need not be physically tired but could be under a lot of stress internally. For example, an impending tough exam, a court case, losing a job, workplace harassment, dealing with irrational people, accepting a heavy responsibility, etc., can create a lot of stress. On the other hand, plain tiredness, usually caused by excessive physical activity or exercise, can be eliminated by a few hours of sound sleep or a good hot bath. But stress cannot be eliminated by sleep or a bath.

Often, people under duress will not be able to identify or sometimes admit the precise reason for their stress and start feeling the whole world is ganging up on them. Over time, stressed people will soon be unable to explain exactly why they are stressed. They feel attacked from all sides, feel unlucky and exhausted, and start getting agitated at everything, trivial, big, related, or unrelated. And the standard reasons people give for stress will be vague and generic stuff like work pressure, traffic, noise, politics, etc. But pointing fingers at vague and subjective stuff does not help you in finding workable solutions. You need to be exact. But how exactly do you pinpoint your stress generator without visiting a stress management consultant? Just use a simple technique called ASKING QUESTIONS TO YOURSELF, similar to what consultants and doctors do when you go for a consultation. Through appropriate and pertinent questions to yourself, it's actually possible to identify your stress generators and often eliminate or control them on your own without external help.

So, whenever you are stressed in the workplace, start asking yourself the following questions. You can add more questions, if necessary, but this exhaustive list should be enough to begin.

- Are the job requirements absolutely clear in real-world terms for what you are trying to do, or expected of you? Or are you simply chasing hype and jargon?
- Do you have the necessary tools, knowledge, resources, staffing, training, and budgets to do what you are trying to do?
- Are the timeframes realistic for whatever you are trying to do, or are you chasing artificial

deadlines created by clueless people? Are you burning out chasing unrealistic expectations from impatient customers, end users, bosses, etc.?

- Are you working in a humorless department or organization?

- Are you generally short-tempered and impatient by nature? Do you habitually get flared up over trivial workplace issues? Are others expecting you to read their mind and act accordingly? Alternatively, do you expect others to read your mind and act accordingly?

- Is it a specific colleague(s) who is the cause of your stress, or is somebody constantly breathing down your neck? Is someone out to get you, discredit you, or snatch the credit for your efforts?

- Are somebody's short temper and irrational behavior preventing you from doing or saying the right things?

- Are you having financial difficulties? Do you have no control over your spending? Are you spending more than you are earning?

- Is a corporate rumor about getting fired, downsizing, reorganization, etc., causing stress?

- Do you have to do everything yourself? Are you getting the required help from your colleagues and other departments? Are you always trying to go out of your way to get things done? Are you trying to tackle things that are not in your control?

- Is the work you are doing really difficult, or are you just dealing with difficult and irrational customers and bosses who create panic and terror to cover up their inadequacies?

- Are you worrying about something that happened in the past or may happen in the future?

- Do you have any known health problems that could be causing stress? Have you had a complete health check-up to detect hidden health disorders? Is a family member's health or behavior creating stress and agitation in the workplace?

Identify Your Stress Triggers

- Are you trying to reinvent the wheel in getting a job done? Can you get tips, procedures, and suggestions from someone who has done such things already?

- Is your life controlled by emails, pagers, mobile phones, blogs, iPods, laptops, and other electronic leashes?

- Are you working on a badly managed project? Is everything in your organization or department urgent and chaotic due to poor planning, an impatient boss, etc.? Is your department understaffed and overworked?

- Are you taking care of your health and rest properly? Are you getting your eight hours of calm sleep daily?

- Are you trying to please or seek admiration from everyone? Are you an appreciation-seeking addict? Is somebody's urgency or poor planning an emergency for you?

- Do you wear uncomfortable and tight clothes to work? Uncomfortable clothes, tight neckties, and certain nylon materials can often cause a lot of fatigue and agitation without you realizing why.

- Are you bad at time management? Are there too many things on your plate? Can you ignore or eliminate the unnecessary ones?

- Are family problems creating hell at work? Are work problems creating hell at home?

- Do you have too much work? Do you have very little or no work? Very little work can also create anxiety about the continuity of your job.

And the questions can go on, or depending on the nature of your work the list of questions can change. But as you can see, precision questions like the above can often pinpoint the exact cause of your stress. Next, eliminating that stress will be in the precise answers you can provide, solutions you can gather, or the specific actions you can take to reduce them. The solutions may not drop in overnight, but you can definitely find solutions over time to switch to the right stress reduction lane gradually.

And we can conclude this chapter with two beautiful quotes on questions by Anthony Robbins.

'Questions provide the key to unlocking our unlimited potential.'

'Successful people ask better questions, and as a result, they get better answers.'

Happy self-interrogation.

When the Hard Way is the Easy Way

Few stories have gained wide fame in the way a small inspirational story of 'The Star Thrower' written by the late scientist Loren Eiseley has. The story is like this. There was once a wise man who used to go to the beach frequently to get ideas for his writing. One day, as he was walking, he saw someone throwing something into the sea. As he got closer, he saw a young man picking up starfish and gently throwing them into the ocean.

The wise man asked, 'Young man, what are you doing?' The young man replied, 'Throwing starfish into the water. The sun is rising, and the tide is out. If I don't throw them in, they will dehydrate and die.' For this, the wise man said, 'But don't you realize that there are miles of beach and thousands of starfish all along it? You can't possibly make a difference!' The young man bent down again and picked up another starfish and threw it into the sea. Next, turning to the wise man he said, 'See, it made a difference for that one.'

This simple starfish story has been widely used in many corporate leadership lessons about the power within each one of us to make a positive difference to others. And this story can also be interpreted in a different way where the wise man is unconsciously seeking the perfect solution to throw all the starfish into the sea in one go, rather than the clumsy way of doing it one by one. He sees no easy way to cover miles and miles of scattered starfish, and the tiny effort of picking one by one seems basically futile and tiresome. And since it's a never-ending exercise, why even attempt such a job and strain yourself?

As normal people, most of us would instantly agree with this argument. Naturally, it's quite common to refuse, avoid, and grumble about anything that takes a long time, is inefficient, is not automatic, needs too many steps, does not have a final everlasting solution, etc. However, there are ample reasons why one should not wait for the perfect solution or grumble about the lack of perfection or clarity in anything we do.

Firstly, perfection and making things elegant is a costly business. While the pursuit of perfection is not a crime, it may often be unachievable. For example, to make something perfect or extremely simple for everyone to use (or afford), tons of money may have to be spent. Simplicity is often very expensive. Hence, a mediocre way that is readily available for use now can often out beat a perfect way that is still unknown or light years away. So, a mediocre way that produces at least a handful of results at the end of the day is far better than not doing anything at all or waiting for someone to invent the perfect way. As Mother Teresa used to say, 'Don't wait for leaders. Do it person to person.' All great cooks, doctors, artists, surgeons, lawyers, and teachers know and practice this simple philosophy.

Theodore Roosevelt once said, 'Do what you can, with what you have, where you are.' Often, in many areas, an imperfect, clumsy, hard, or goofy method is the only way possible to get things done. But people often live in an illusionary world believing everything can be done in several excellent ways to ease the burden on humankind. And it's common to argue that there must be a better way or many spectacular ways of doing a particular activity. True, a single piece of work or activity can theoretically be done in many flamboyant ways. But the harsh reality is that the mediocre way is probably the only viable way in the given circumstances, compulsions, and limitations. For example, while dealing with bureaucratic governments you must go through a series of outdated processes that don't make sense no matter how much you grumble. But if you don't follow their method, you don't get your work done. So, if you have to fill sixteen lengthy forms by hand in triplicate to get something done, you have to do it, though you can endlessly argue about a better system, implement computers, web-enabled, click of a button, etc.

Somebody once said, *'The path to perfection leads to procrastination. Don't let perfect ruin good.'* While seeking the perfect solution for something is not a crime, not attempting anything till that perfect solution is visualized or found is dumb. A perfection paralysis often stops you from starting any work. People often fear announcing or executing a half-baked plan because it attracts ridicule. So, the risk of being laughed at freezes people into taking no action at all, or just waiting perpetually. But nothing would get done at all if one waited till someone could do it so well that no one can find any fault with it. So, even if that ultimate solution is a million miles away, it's better to start something however small it may seem.

Finally, we can conclude this chapter with a great quote from Lee Iacocca who said, *'I have always found that if I move with seventy-five percent or more of the facts that I usually never regret it. It's the guys who wait to have everything perfect that drive you crazy.'*

Unusual Cures for Boring Meetings

It is not even 10:00 am on Monday and it's already time to rush into one of those dreadful weekly status report meetings, a ritual that started sometime in your previous birth. You know for sure that no one will have anything substantial to report, or a few trumpeters will hype up their trivial tasks, or someone will hijack the whole meeting, or a few egos will get bruised, and the meetings will go on till eternity or until your bladders burst. Besides, those umpteen cups of coffee, tea, and biscuits are fast taking you many steps closer to indigestion and ulcers. Every day, millions of people waste time on useless meetings that serve no purpose.

And nonstop meetings are one of the most life-draining and unavoidable activities of the corporate world, standing only next to performance appraisals in toxicity. In many organizations, a stage has been reached where the very mention of the word meeting is equated with something boring and life-draining. Today, many managers and employees go to the office just to attend meetings throughout the day without getting a chance to do any meaningful work. For example, in some organizations even the most trivial of tasks cannot be done without first calling a meeting, then a second meeting, and countless other meetings. Agreed, meetings and conference calls are necessary to run things, but instead of running things they usually end up stopping things from happening. Also, another big challenge for the meeting initiators is to keep all the attendees awake.

Thinking out of the box, have you ever asked yourself why all team meetings have to revolve only around status reports, reorganizations, metrics, jargon-filled presentations, performance appraisals, process improvements, customer complaints, finding scapegoats, etc.? Well, you may loudly argue that is what the business is all about. So, meetings are necessary whether people like it or not. True, some meetings are unavoidable and absolutely necessary to run the business. But as a manager in charge of leading (and sometimes inspiring) a team, what can you do to make your team meetings more enjoyable, knowledge-oriented, and almost a pure joy for everyone? What is the magic pill to make meetings more exciting, produce better results, and gradually eliminate the need for routine meetings?

It is quite simple. Have more meetings, but of a different variety. Apart from essential departmental meetings, periodically have at least 20–30% of your team meetings that have nothing to do with your business or customer issues.

Now you may again loudly argue that you are not paid by your management or the customer to do such meetings as they have nothing to do with the business. Besides, who will have time or money for all that stuff? But the unique meetings I am going to recommend can take you to a different dimension of business improvement and people management skills, well beyond the dry fodder that is fed as management best practices everywhere.

Have a look at the topics suggested below.

Inspirational Quotes Meeting: Have a meeting where you read, enjoy, and discuss hundreds of great, inspirational quotes of various leaders around the world. Such quotes contain wisdom and advice that has withstood the test of time. Many quotes contain fantastic management wisdom. There have been numerous cases where a single inspirational quote has completely changed the life of many people. For example, a quote like, 'It is a terrible thing to look over your shoulder when you are trying to lead and find no one there - Franklin Roosevelt,' or 'There will be a time when loud-mouthed, incompetent people will seem to be getting the best of you. When that happens, you only have to be patient and wait for them to self-destruct. It never fails - Richard Rybolt,' can start a very interesting conversation and self-awareness.

Stress Management Meeting: Discuss and brainstorm useful and practicable stress management techniques that can be practiced within and outside the workplace. For example, a simple technique like a proper breathing exercise can be a great knowledge and productivity enhancer for the team to deal with stress caused by various workplace issues.

Life of a Great Leader Meeting: Have a meeting where you study the life of one or more great world nonbusiness leaders and freedom fighters like Lincoln, Churchill, Gandhi, Mother Teresa, Rosa Parks, or even Hitler. The lives of nonbusiness leaders around the world and the kind of troubles they have endured can have a terrific impact on your life. For example, the perseverance of Nelson Mandela, who spent 27 years rotting in jail, can make you feel like your workplace troubles are nothing compared to what some people have suffered.

Gift a Book Meeting: Most employees, including managers, don't read good books relating to management, history, religion, self-help, etc. This is why there are so many workplace problems worldwide. But reading and re-reading a good book can take you to a different level of professionalism, confidence, and business improvement techniques that can help both the business and the individual. For example, have your team members gift each other a good self-help or management book by investing ten or twenty dollars every two months.

Family and Health Issues Meeting: Have a meeting that can openly discuss family problems and health tips. People often avoid discussing family and personal health issues openly as they consider it washing dirty linen in public. But if you can overcome that strong inertia and slowly start discussing whatever is discussable, it can often provide valuable insights into a person's behavior and understanding each other. Each employee is unique with his or her own personal problems that can impact their style of work. For example, in a lighter sense, employees with no kids can perhaps understand why employees with naughty kids grow bald faster or cannot take work home. Often, nobody knows or admits openly that the health condition of an employee's family member can also play an important role in an employee's concentration and productivity in an organization.

People often think that employees should leave their family problems in their homes. But it's neither that easy nor humane to ignore family issues, as everyone will have some pressing problem or the other. Such issues can have a serious impact on a person's overall concentration, productivity, and contribution to an organization. For example, I have seen how a young team member of mine lost his concentration and interest in work due to his parent's terminal disease that lasted for nearly two years. But the question you should ask is whether such an employee can be punished for poor performance or should the team pitch in to lift his or her spirits and take teamwork to the next generation.

Financial Planning Meeting: Discuss ways in which team members can learn and enforce proper financial planning in their lives. Various studies have proved that most people know nothing about proper financial planning or its importance. They could be getting a great salary but saving practically nothing. But when the Damocles sword falls on their head it will be too late to do anything. You need to save for a rainy day to prevent serious trouble for yourself and your dependents and family members. Similar to an organization's disaster recovery and business continuity plans, you need to have a personal disaster recovery and livelihood continuity plan. Enough money in the bank and other safe investments provides you with that much-needed mental strength to handle workplace harassment, including job losses. Anything unexpected may happen to you at any time, and that is why it's important to save some money for emergencies through proper financial planning.

Work-Life Balance Meeting: Discuss ways in which you can enforce work-life balance to improve everyone's health. Today, everyone talks about work-life balance, but nothing substantial happens in any department. In my umpteen years in the workplace, I have never come across any real management-sponsored mechanism to reduce stress and improve the health of employees. And I have never seen any HR representative walk across the floors and chase employees out at 5:00 pm or on weekends so that they go home to enjoy a proper work-life balance.

Hobbies Meeting: Discuss hobbies and interests of team members. You may be surprised to know the existence of great talent within your own teams that can be exploited and nurtured for mutual benefit.

Video Meetings: Today, excellent DVDs are available containing speeches, presentations, and coaching sessions on a variety of business and self-help topics prepared by management gurus and reputed authors. Normally, such videos are expensive but worth every penny as they can be very interesting and highly educational. Every department library should have a good collection of such DVDs, and periodic video sessions can be arranged for the benefit of all your team members. Similarly, countless beneficial topics like email etiquette, humor and harassment in the workplace, handling rude customers, charity, useful electronic gadgets, household tips, first aid, and even philosophy, etc., can be discussed to everyone's benefit.

Each of the above topics has the indirect potential to help the employee as well as the business. Very soon, the knowledge gained in such meetings can pay rich dividends, both to the employee and the organization. They can also inject a superior level of self-consciousness that can help you inside and outside the workplace, and also gradually reduce the need for moronic business meetings. Get suggestions from various employees for unique topics. Always try to choose topics that can attract many people without much prodding. But not everyone may be interested in every topic. If somebody is not interested in a particular topic, then don't force them. Keep the duration short, sweet, and at moderate intervals like once a month to make every meeting a refreshing and memorable one.

Now, who would like to attend an exciting meeting on, *'Fungus wilt caused on Pseudomonas Solanacearum by Calonectria and Cylindrocladium Spathiphylli bacteria in eastern Cambodia?'* ☺

Top Myths and Facts about Teamwork

A general dictionary defines teamwork as a *'Cooperative or coordinated effort on the part of a group of persons acting together in the interests of a common cause, unison for a higher cause, or people working together for a selfless purpose, and so on.'* Applied to workplaces, teamwork is a method that aligns employee mindsets in a cooperative (and supposedly selfless) manner toward a specific business purpose. Today, there is no organization that does not talk about the need and value of teamwork in their workplaces.

And there is no dearth of management gurus who argue and describe the immense benefits of teamwork. However, while the concept of teamwork and its benefits are well known and talked about, it's very rare to see it being practiced in reality. And secondly, what you may have noticed outwardly as teamwork is not really teamwork internally. To understand why, you need to first be aware of a few myths and facts about teamwork, and why it does not work in reality, or cannot be sustained for a long time.

Human nature: Human beings are fiercely independent animals and will always have their own opinions and independent methods of doing something, though they may be unwilling to express them openly. This is the way we humans are hardwired by nature for millions of years. Except for a very small percentage of people, sharing and collaboration with others are not exactly programmed inside every human being.

This is because each person is mainly concerned about his or her rewards, appreciation, need for power over others, and so on. But teamwork insists on everyone playing an unnatural ballgame that aligns our mindsets in a cooperative and usually selfless manner toward a specific business purpose. And this involves unpalatable stuff like sacrifices, compromises, sharing of rewards, sharing blame and punishments, suppression of personal opinions, etc., which is not acceptable to almost anyone. No matter what is expressed on the outside, internally it's always, 'What is in it for me?' rather than, 'What is in it for us?'

The illusion of teamwork: A popular proverb says birds of the same feather flock together. Groups and crowds are often mistaken for teams. Employees form groups, crowds, mobs, and unions for personal reasons and desires. For example, it's quite natural for people belonging to the same religion, speaking the same language, belonging to a certain ethnic group, sharing the same bad habits (or hobbies), sharing a common enemy, studying in the same college, etc., to stick together. But they don't really become a team. And again, just because a bunch of employees stick together for lunch, cigarettes, boozing, movies, rag juniors, have wild parties, indulge in idle gossip, etc., does not mean they have actually formed a great team.

That is just a mob at work or marriages of convenience formed mainly for personal reasons and interests. This illusion of togetherness is often mistaken for teamwork. But the underlying reason people collaborate is that they believe it's in their personal interest to do so, and not for a higher selfless purpose. In reality, what usually unites people are mainly common fears and limitations. They see safety in numbers and behave in a similar fashion. For example, employees at junior levels easily stick together to help and assist each other because they are bound by common fears and limitations. The common fears and limitations are things like young age, lack of knowledge, experience, power, etc., which do not allow them to survive independently yet. Even historically, for centuries kings with small kingdoms would form diplomatic partnerships with other small kingdoms, not because they wanted to form a team. They united because they believed by combining their powers they could prevent an attack by a bigger or more powerful common enemy.

The lifespan of teamwork: Teamwork, even when it works in rare cases, always has a limited lifespan. Continuing the above example, once people grow up and get the required experience, knowledge, and money power, you will rarely see them stick together the way they used to do before. For example, kids are always close to their parents when they are small. But once they grow up and gain worldly experience, they hardly depend on their parents anymore and will even oppose them at every opportunity. Similarly, once employees gain more knowledge, more money, more clout, more talent, more seniority, etc., they will rarely want to work as a team bound by a common purpose.

Instead, they start seeing themselves as independent advisors and decision-makers and want to lead a team toward their perceived directions of success, and not work inside a team led by someone else. This is why you rarely see teams at the top layers of management, or with professors, doctors, lawyers, etc., and instead, only see icy jealousies and cold wars for power and prestige.

People behavior during success and failure: The true colors of people can be seen when there is a reward or punishment to be shared. When something succeeds, you definitely see and hear a lot of noise about teamwork and how they pulled it together as a team. For example, when a project, task, or activity succeeds, then suddenly every Tom, Dick, and Harry will join the bandwagon to share the laurels and a piece of the cake. But if the same project, task, or activity fails miserably, the group will never lift their hands together in unison to share the blame. This will not be seen even in employee groups that earlier used to shout the loudest claiming they were a great team. Instead, the first thing that will definitely happen is to find one or more scapegoats to pin the blame on.

The need for it: Often, people who give sermons on teamwork will rarely work as a team themselves if given a choice. For example, politicians are the ones who talk the most about teamwork. They always like to have a large number of people with them because they need a large number of votes to win. If the rules of winning in democratic politics were somehow changed and did not depend on the high number of votes, you would never see any politician talking about teamwork.

Finally, we can conclude this chapter with a quote about teamwork from Michael Winner who said, *'A team effort is a lot of people doing what I say.'*

Workaholics are Not Role Models

A CEO of a reputed organization once said he has been working more than 90 to 100 hours a week for many years, and jokingly added he should have done more. And in another reputed car manufacturing company, dozens of employees and managers get cash rewards and appreciation certificates for not taking a single day's leave during the last two or three years. In yet another case, a jet-set CEO was proudly patting his own back, stating that he loves his work so much that he often does not see his family or kids for several weeks and cannot remember when he took a couple of days' leave or a vacation.

Nowadays, the number of such morons is increasing at an exponential rate. And you can very easily spot such people as they will be constantly talking on their mobiles, checking their handheld devices for text messages, or always connected to their office via their laptops for never-ending emails and so on. Such people have their hands and minds loaded with projects, countless unfinished tasks, endless meetings, emails, and constantly sweating the small, medium, and big details. When questioned, they claim to enjoy their job so much that they just work, work, and do more work, especially to impress the media. And they also proudly believe they can be role models for others. However, contrary to what they believe or self-congratulate, such habits are nothing to be proud of, nor should they be your role models, as you will shortly see. In reality, workaholics are always driven by deep internal needs rather than external ones. Here are some ugly facts about workaholics.

A New York tour operator once proudly said, 'New York is a city that never sleeps.' For this, an elderly tourist calmly replied, 'And it definitely looks like it.' Super workaholics are not necessarily the most efficient people, even if they stubbornly work 18 hours a day. In fact, they are the least efficient of people. They may appear to be working, but internally their brain would have turned off. The output they produce or the ideas they generate when the brain and essential body systems turn off is nothing but trash and mediocre stuff.

Workaholics often believe themselves to be perfectionists and role models, and often the media also portrays them as so. But in reality, they are neither perfectionists nor can be role models to anyone sensible and knowledgeable about the hazards of overwork. They may have plenty of hollow followers who are as lunatic as themselves, but no sensible person will agree with or appreciate this kind of burnout.

High workaholics suffer from a disease called **obsessive compulsive disorder** and an inability to let go. Most of them suffer from the indispensability syndrome to constantly prove something great every day and every minute. They cannot bear being left out and always want to be involved in everything. They are terrified of being left out of the loop or some information. They are unable to delegate. And they believe nothing can work if they are not involved.

Excessive workaholics are appreciation-seeking addicts with a deep craving for recognition and appreciation. They suffer from a deep inferiority complex and try to cover it up by proving they can work long hours and days without a break. Just like drugs, once a person gets into the appreciation-seeking habit, it's very difficult for them to stop. They constantly seek appreciation and will keep doing things to invite more appreciation, even if their mind and body refuse to tag along.

Working non-stop is perhaps the lousiest of work habits and work-life balance. It is also the perfect road to ruining your health and that of others. Poor health and lack of solid family life lead to poor performance and relationships at work. Workaholics not only ruin their health but also that of their subordinates and their family members. Of course, they may earn more money than ordinary workers and access more materialistic pleasures. But when they get a heart attack, stroke, high blood pressure, and other nervous disorders, it's their family and dependents who will bear the brunt of looking after a human vegetable. Hence, every workplace and home needs mentally and physically balanced individuals who can create pleasantness instead of chaos, stress, and constant pressure.

Workaholics often don't know whether they are workaholics. They falsely believe they are role models to the younger generation or their peers. But people will often pretend to appreciate a workaholic in front of them, while they laugh and ridicule them behind their back.

Finally, no one on their deathbed ever says, 'I wish I could have worked more.'

And we can conclude this chapter with a great quote from Bertrand Russell, *'One of the symptoms of an approaching nervous breakdown is the belief that one's work is terribly important.'*

Why Some People Drive You Nuts

An ancient proverb says, 'Everyone looks normal until you get to know them better.' And the reverse is also true, that is, *'Everyone looks abnormal until you get to know them better.'* On our planet, a very large percentage of people exhibit characteristics of being tough, highly independent, stubborn, impossible to please, restless, perfectionists, etc., and they continue to lead their entire life like that. Practically, everyone would have definitely experienced or heard true stories of such people who drive others nuts through their irrational behaviors. The traditional methods of interaction that work for normal or sweet people just don't work for them. So, how do you deal with such tough people?

The simple answer is you cannot in most cases. Nor can you fully blame the other person for acting irrational, as there is usually a scientific reason for such behavior. And that reason is biological in nature, as man is not a uniformly programmed species like animals and birds. As you would have observed, animals and birds of a species behave in exactly the same manner. For example, a sheep has been biologically programmed by Mother Nature to be a timid creature, while a tiger has been programmed to be ferocious. You don't see tigers give up their ferocious nature even if you breed and train them in captivity. And a sheep cannot be trained to become a ferocious creature. But no such rules apply to human beings. Man is not uniform in his behavior, and each person is unique in his or her own inborn ways.

For example, even in the case of identical twins, one can exhibit a rough nature while another can be sweet. This is why it's rarely possible to effectively lead people unless you use some unconventional methods. Or it's better to gain the specific knowledge that teaches you how to understand why people act cranky. Coming back to the original discussion, people who are restless, impatient, irritable, tough, perfectionists, demanding, etc., normally belong to a category called Type-A personality, or in some cases can be a higher version called Type-A+, the kind you see in dictators or extremely tough and dangerous people.

In fact, Type-A/A+ personality develops right from childhood, and this is why we see many kids are difficult to handle. It's not easy to deal with Type-A/A+ people for the simple reason you could be one yourself. Most people don't know they are Type-A unless a doctor or psychologist tells them. It is this lack of knowledge that causes a great deal of grief both ways when dealing with such people. Nevertheless, it's important to recognize that a mysterious feature called a Type-A/A+ personality exists in many humans and learn some ways to deal with it effectively. Given below is a layman's guide to understanding the characteristics of Type A and A+ people.

Type-A people suffer from an exaggerated sense of urgency for everything. For example, they hate being late or being kept waiting. They periodically experience bouts of anger, restlessness, irritability, impatience, and general hostility toward everything. Due to this, they get angry for simple or even trivial reasons without realizing why.

Such people don't know how and when to relax and are always in an endless state of internal turmoil, often uncontrolled and unknowingly. Their thinking and thoughts will normally be very intense. They are usually very independent and direct to the point. For example, they don't take insults or criticism lightly.

They will always be on the lookout for perfection (of their definition) in everything they do. Such people demand that perfection even from others and want everyone to rise to their level of thinking and working. They expect others to read their mind and act accordingly, thereby making others uncomfortable and often exhibiting dictatorial behaviors.

Facial calmness is different from internal turmoil. Internally they will experience enormous amounts of personal stress that they cannot release easily or share with others. Such people don't realize their effect on others as they simply do not see the ugly picture they portray.

Type-A people also experience higher degrees of heart troubles than others.

If you are a Type-A person yourself: The most important knowledge in life is to constantly be aware of your own behaviors. Before criticizing or grumbling about the qualities of others, it's important to test if you belong to a Type-A/A+ personality yourself. For this, you need a candid discussion with yourself or perhaps a doctor to see if you have any of the qualities mentioned above. Secondly, there are some psychological tests available free on the internet that can determine if you are a Type-A/A+, provided you answer the questions honestly. If you discover you are a Type-A/A+, then you should take immediate steps to create an internal calmness program before you go bust. The change will not happen overnight, but now that you know a beast exists inside you, it's time to take charge of your behaviors and not let it run amok. For example, the next time you start getting impatient when waiting for someone or something, you can realize the nasty agitation that is brewing inside you is because you have a Type-A personality. Then you can start calming down and stop getting agitated further.

Gradually, you will understand why you are stressed, why you are always agitated, why you blow your fuse, why you can't relax, and so on. Soon, for every irrational behavior you exhibit, you can have immediate self-realization gently thumping you on the head to steer you to calmer behavior. Armed with this knowledge, you can now gradually learn to relax, be lazy, cultivate the power to let go, and enjoy life better.

If you are dealing with a Type-A person: Except for a genuine mental illness and certain types of personal problems, it's usually the intense biological forces of Type-A/A+ that make people act cranky for anything and everything. But if you are knowledgeable about the characteristics of a Type-A/A+ person, it's easy to understand the irrational behavior of others. So, if a person is acting impatient or fussy, you now know exactly why they do that. Instead of agitating the person further, you can think of ways to help him or her if possible. And you can also educate them to realize they are a Type-A/A+ person so that it enlightens them and others.

There is another personality called a Type-B personality, or a socializer type, who has the following characteristics:

They are relaxed and have a cool attitude.

They are friendly, patient, easy to deal with, and generally content with life.

They will be at peace and harmony within themselves, positively look at life, and are not too concerned about losing.

Finally, your objective is to gradually become a Type-B person to a large extent in your life, while retaining the Type-A behaviors in areas where it's absolutely necessary. It's not easy to make the jump from A/A+ to B and may take several months of conscious effort, but it's possible if you take small sustained steps toward it.

Finally, we conclude this chapter with a beautiful quote from Lao Tzu who said, *'Nature never hurries, yet everything is accomplished.'*

Biorhythms – Your Biological Batteries

Have you ever observed that you feel bubbly and full of energy on certain days, and feel exactly the opposite and low on some days? You observe doing an astonishing amount of work when you are feeling high and also observe that you don't feel like doing the same productive work when you are down, even though you are not sick or really tired. And you may have also observed that these high and low feelings can last inside you for several days. So, what is this cycle of highs and lows that you experience periodically? And how come you see many people claim to be always energetic, excited, and passionate about everything, every minute, and every hour, while you personally feel lazy and unenergetic periodically? What is their superhuman secret that you are unaware of?

Secondly, with all the energetic individuals around, how can you honestly blurt out that you don't feel excited about that yet one more boring meeting on customer satisfaction when you are feeling low? Now, how do you prove to everyone that you can also be excited, energetic, and passionate like them about everything every day? Will special vitamin tablets, daily exercises, power lunches, or even some workplace productivity and enthusiasm-enhancing drugs help? Or is there some other magic to be always active? If you are eagerly expecting me to share some golden solutions to eliminate your low productivity days, then you are going to be disappointed. What I am going to tell you is to do nothing, and simply learn to live with your highs and lows.

Many would normally disagree with my above suggestion and proudly claim that they are always able to maintain a peak physical, mental, and emotional condition every day. But the unfortunate truth is, no matter what you do, the rich food you eat, the books you read, or the calories you pump out, you cannot remain excited, enthusiastic, or energetic every day. Mother Nature has programmed everyone to undergo an endless cycle of active and passive periods in their physical, emotional, and mental states. Whether you believe it or not, you will feel highly energetic and enthusiastic on certain days (active phase) and feel bored, exhausted, weak, irritable, and uninterested in anything on certain days (passive phase). And this cycle of high and low days will happen throughout your lifetime.

The answer to why you feel high or low lies in a relatively unknown and often dismissed concept called biorhythms. At the beginning of the last century, a certain Dr. Wilhelm Fliess noticed identical rhythms in the case histories of his patients. He observed active and passive phases (curves) in the physical, emotional, and mental rhythms of his patients. Based on his observations, he derived the principle of biorhythms and observed that the physical curve spanned 23 days, the emotional curve 28 days, and the mental curve 33 days.

And Hermann Swoboda, a professor of psychology at the University of Vienna, while researching periodic variations in fevers, looked into the possibility of a rhythmic change in the moods and health of people. Based on the data he collected in areas like pain, an outbreak of fevers, illnesses, heart attacks, and recurrent dreams, he concluded that there was a 23-day physical cycle and a 28-day emotional cycle. These curves are usually plotted as sine waves similar to an alternating current we studied in our high schools. A cycle is said to be in a positive phase when above the zero line and in a negative phase when below the zero line. And there are also some mathematical formulas and free online tools that can plot the curves for you based on your birth date and other inputs. However, the core idea behind this chapter is not to make you become some sort of wizard in plotting your biorhythms. Instead, this chapter is to teach how you can successfully exploit your highs and lows.

High days: Assuming that you are not suffering from any serious health problems or other personal headaches that can make you feel low, the trick is to utilize both your active and passive phases to your advantage. You need to become like an ant when you are feeling active. Ants collect food throughout the summer, as they know winter will set in fast. So, they collect the maximum amount of food and other useful material to survive the winter. They know when winter sets in they will not be able to move out or get food easily. Hence, they do not waste their summers by enjoying the sun and loafing around. When winter sets in, they enjoy the fruits of their summer labor.

Similarly, you should aim to do the maximum amount of important work (official and personal) on the days you feel great. This could be anything like finishing off a report that is not due for weeks, attacking all pending workplace issues, organizing your finances, trimming the garden, repairing the roof, cleaning the garage, eliminating the clutter in your house and workplace, and anything that you have been putting off for weeks. On such days you can multitask to do an extraordinary amount of work and still be energetic.

The challenge will be to avoid wasting such days for 'nice to do' things like picnics and sports, or simply waste them by doing things that don't help you in a true sense. The question you should ask yourself is, 'When you are feeling your best, where should you first direct that energy?' For example, do you use that phase to properly organize all your messed-up finances by visiting a financial consultant, or use this time for picnics, ball games, beach trips, and other 'nice to do' stuff, rather than tackle a 'must do' stuff.

Low days: If you have entered your low phase, you may feel guilty because you are wasting precious time without doing anything meaningful. And you may ask why you are unable to concentrate on any work now when just a few days ago you felt great and did a lot of meaningful work. But now your mind and body are simply refusing to pump that vibrant energy juice you need to get things done. And for every effort to do some meaningful work, you feel some invisible force pushing you back. You start making minor and major mistakes, ordinary things will seem like drudgery, and the simplest of tasks will seem Herculean.

However, the key to tackling your low days lies in what you do during your high days. If you have done your best during your high days, then you should simply 'take it easy' during your low days. Just do only the things that you cannot postpone, avoid all critical activities if possible, and don't worry about not having a productive day. On your low days, you are better off listening to signals and resistance from your body and mind that tell you that you are running on low batteries rather than fighting with it. For example, it's believed that some doctors plan their work around their highs and lows, and don't tackle critical surgeries when they are feeling low. And there have been some studies and evidence to prove that drivers meet with accidents more when they are in their low phase rather than high phase.

So, if you are regularly experiencing high and low productive days, now you know the hidden reason and need not feel guilty or worried at all. You are actually in good shape and your biological machinery is in perfect condition. You can proudly say you are a normal human being and not act artificially like many people do to impress others. The question is whether you can honestly admit that you are feeling low when you are indeed feeling low. To summarize, your biological batteries need to continuously charge and discharge. So, get used to accepting your highs and lows and use them to your advantage.

The Power of Reading Management Books

Sometime back while attending a management seminar I was chatting with a fellow manager from a different company. And the discussion gradually drifted to the area of books, especially management books. I asked the person what sort of books he normally reads and pop came his answer something like, 'I don't read any management books. Never had a need for them. They are all theoretical trash.' And a few others around seemed to agree with him by giving their own versions like, 'Who has the time due to heavy workloads, they are too costly, it does not work, they are written by theoretical people who don't know the realities,' and so on.

Their arguments reminded me of the classic story of a lumberjack working hard cutting some wood. A foreman who saw a lumberjack sweating asks why he doesn't sharpen the saw to help speed up his work. The lumberjack answers, 'I can't waste time sharpening my saw because I'm too busy chopping wood.' His answer can be slightly modified to today's managers who claim to read no books as, 'I can't waste my time reading management books because I am too busy doing management.'

There are countless such managers in countless organizations worldwide that don't own or read a single book on management. And they will be trying very hard every day to cover up their lack of management skills by resorting to endless experimentation, often with disastrous results. However, there was a time long ago when management books were too theoretical, as Jack Welch once commented, 'Insecure managers create complexity. Frightened, nervous managers use thick, convoluted planning books.' But that warped thinking was applicable decades ago.

Now the situation has changed drastically. Today, excellent books are available written by great people who have been there, done that, and are not embarrassed to share their positive and negative experiences. Many such books are not impractical theoretical gibberish, and the knowledge in them cannot be simply brushed aside. So, it's up to you to seek that knowledge for your benefit. Some of the top advantages of reading management books are as follows.

They help you commit fewer mistakes due to ignorant experimentation. Managers who have the habit of reading management books, best practices, white papers, etc., have a distinct advantage over managers who claim to do management without this knowledge. For example, a young manager or employee who periodically reads good books can easily outshine a manager having several years more experience without reading books.

You can't be effective in your area of work continuously if you don't sharpen your saw by improving your academic skills or knowledge in your area of work. And that can only be gained by reading books, no matter how many people you know. Today, if anyone proudly claims they don't read management books, they are only fooling themselves. And they will also end up doing something worse. With their half-baked knowledge about management and ignoring the advice from good books, they will only do more harm than good.

Books help you avoid reinventing the wheel. You avoid committing the mistakes others have experienced. Worldwide, people experience similar or identical problems related to managing people, businesses, customers, etc. So, if someone else has experienced a set of troubles, solved them, and made that knowledge available to others, then you should greedily suck that advice to your advantage.

It's not necessarily the ones that sell millions of copies that contain great management advice. Every management book (even mediocre ones) has several good takeaways if you know what to read and what to skip.

You learn the do's and don'ts faster irrespective of whether you get a chance to experience every tricky management situation. You can easily give better advice to others. The knowledge you gain by reading one good management book is equivalent to many years of practical experience contaminated with dozens of blunders and goof-ups.

Reading books regularly can also help you to de-stress easily, and soon you will also gradually experience a stark difference in the way you think, act, and behave. Many books have the power to change your life. Like tiny homeopathic medicines, the gems of wisdom in every book can make you calmer, handle criticism, understand mankind better, and become well equipped to tackle life's ups and downs.

Readers are leaders, and many top performers read a book chapter or a new useful article every day. Reading good management and self-help books is a quick way to gain many years of experience from a few hours of study. By learning some speed reading, you can absorb large quantities of information in relatively small periods of time.

The more you know, the less you need to fear. Knowledge is power. However, do not take everything said in the book as heavenly advice. Only take whatever useful ideas you need or can practice. Not all chapters are worth reading, and even great popular books contain many mediocre and bland chapters. But each book will have at least one useful tool or takeaway. So, take what you need and what works for you, and discard what doesn't help you.

And we can conclude this chapter with a few great quotes about books.

'Books are the carriers of civilization. Without books, history is silent, literature dumb, science

crippled, thought and speculation at a standstill.'
Barbara Tuchman

'Some books are to be tasted, others to be swallowed, and some few to be chewed and digested.' Francis Bacon

Humor – The Ultimate Leadership Style

In today's workplace, the number of problem-related words like 'stress-related illness,' 'burnout,' and 'work-life balance' has become quite common. What this simply means is organizations are at last recognizing the importance of such things. If you have noticed, today's hectic workplaces have become extremely humorless, sapping the energy of everyone right from the janitor to the CEO. For example, when was the last time you had some continuous weeks or months of fun and humor in the office?

However, I am not talking about those occasional and rare humorous situations of exchanging some silly jokes or laughing at a Dilbert cartoon, but a continuous period of workplace enjoyment when you did not dread that Monday morning alarm. A period when you used to go home relaxed and content instead of planning to update your resume. Probably never. But do you remember the amount of fun you used to have as kids? As children, you would laugh or giggle dozens of times an hour. But as you grew up, the laughter reduced dramatically. By the time you became 30 years old, good laughter and fun had disappeared totally. You started avoiding humor and fun as childish stuff. Soon the fun was totally gone from your life, and all you thought about was becoming more and more serious to an extent that a frown could result in a lawsuit.

Everyone knows modern work is often associated with excessive stress and is one of the main causes of illness, absenteeism, and burnout of employees. But until a few years ago, things like sickness, boredom, stress, fatigue, etc., were always considered an employee's personal problem, and the organization was quick to distance itself from the employee's sufferings. In other words, organizations were covering up their lousy leadership skills by blaming their employees for being bad workers. But that thinking has now gradually changed, and professional organizations now accept blame for their employees' stress and are taking active steps to self-correct by introducing fun and laughter at work. However, many ordinary and mediocre organizations still consider humor at work abominable and a distraction from getting the 'real' job done. They do not see the importance of fun in the overall success of their organizations.

But, unknown to many employees and managers, humor is a fantastic stress reliever. In fact, humor is one of the sixty-four qualities of a king. Most people are unaware of the positive effects of humor in the workplace, offices, and homes. People often tend to think humor and laughter are unproductive or unprofessional, and that being serious is the only way to live. This is exactly why you have too many serious managers, serious meetings, work under a high-pressure atmosphere, etc., and finally achieve burnout, ulcers, toxicity, lawsuits, etc.

Actually, humor is not about taking your work, job, and responsibilities lightly, but about seeing the fun in everything you do. It is the ability to laugh and make fun of yourself. It is about creating a pleasant atmosphere where you work and allowing others to give their best without the fear of being reprimanded or punished. And people who work with humorous bosses and managers tend to become highly efficient and productive employees. They can share good news and bad news without fear, and it builds trust both ways. The most successful CEOs are the ones who have discovered the power of clean humor in their day-to-day life, inside and outside the workplace. It's comparable to children who enjoy and learn their studies better when they have a jolly teacher instead of a teacher who is strict and suffocating.

Bruce Baum, a professor at Buffalo State University who specializes in applied and therapeutic humor, says, 'The more fun you have, the more you can get done.' Humor makes everyone feel good and humane. A sense of humor sees the fun in everyday experiences, and appropriate humor can lighten up even extremely difficult situations many times. Management often associates humor with circus jokers. But a humorous person is neither a joker nor a clown. Humor is different from practical jokes, wearing a funny hat, having a red nose, mimicry, or making fun of someone's physical appearance, height, weight, religion, or color. The humor I am talking about is your pleasantness quotient. In other words, how approachable are you? How do you take bad news? Do you shoot the messenger? Do people avoid approaching you for help? Are you a fault inventor? Do you know how to ask beautiful questions? Do people consider you pleasant or toxic? Do you know how to laugh at yourself? And so on. However, it's important to realize that some things like practical jokes are inappropriate and not funny. For example, deleting somebody's important computer files or teasing about their height or skin color is not funny or called humor. Humor is medicine with good taste, but practical jokes are poison and sour. Having fun on the job can stimulate your creative thinking, prevent burnout, and increase productivity.

Various studies have shown that humorous employees are more productive and efficient than workers who work in a stifled, serious atmosphere. Today, many corporations are hiring corporate humorists to bring fun to workplaces. Humor helps one think in different ways, and one should get into the habit of looking for humor in everyday situations. Finally, clean humor is eco-friendly, non-toxic, childproof, and recyclable. Start spreading it.

And we can conclude this chapter with a quote that says, *'If you don't have a sense of humor, you probably don't have any sense at all.'*

The Dicey Art of Escalation

A general dictionary defines escalation in many ways like, *'Increase in intensity, magnitude, bypassing the immediate person, and so on.'* Applied to our workplaces, escalation is usually a formal process in many IT and non-IT projects. For example, if certain employees are unable or unwilling to do a certain activity they are accountable for, then it's necessary for customers to escalate the issue to their superiors for resolution. However, escalation is not a simple or easy-to-use affair in most workplaces, though it can be easily mentioned in policies, processes, and reports. This is because escalation is an instantaneous conflict and vendetta creator as it's often considered a complaint against people.

Another downside is it leads to backlash and revenge as people normally don't take escalations professionally. Hence, many employees and customers often hesitate to escalate pressing issues and concerns to higher-ups fearing a backlash or the wrath of the person. Or they simply give up and suffer in silence. Many a time, junior and new employees even take the blame on themselves or make excuses on behalf of someone, as they will not have the courage to escalate against experienced seniors and toxic employees who deliberately hold up things. Nevertheless, escalation is necessary and must be done as without it many activities just don't happen. So, one must cultivate the habit of escalation whenever and wherever necessary provided the necessary homework is done before escalating. Here are a few ways to do it.

Before rushing to escalate on someone you need to ensure that the necessary formalities and homework are done. Many impatient people are too quick to escalate to all and sundry but conveniently fail to adhere to their portion of responsibilities. For example, a department may initiate action only if a certain work form is filled and handed over to them. But if you have not done that, and instead escalate the issue to their superiors, then you are just asking for trouble because it will simply backfire on you.

Suppose you have done your part and the other party still does not respond, then you may need to prod or remind them formally and gently for some action. In some cases, certain departments will be so busy and short-staffed that nothing can happen even after the necessary formalities and reminders. In such cases, you need to take a call on how to get things done without adding to their misery.

In many organizations, there exists a small percentage of troublemakers who procrastinate and hold things up without rhyme or reason. Such people don't return calls or respond to emails, reminders, etc. And they don't value other people's time, effort, or money. A Chinese proverb says, 'The mountains are tall, and the kind emperor is far away.' Such people misuse this proverbial loophole and thrive because they are sure that people will not escalate against them because of their powers or the unavailability of senior managers who can take action against them.

Such people have the potential to destroy projects, lose customers, cause various grievances, give rude replies, and invent flimsy faults to put the ball back in your court. Or they switch their charm on and off depending on whom they are dealing with. In such cases, the only option is to ensure you escalate to their higher-ups and even higher, provided you have ensured your portion of the homework is complete.

And if they retaliate, you should escalate even that so that they know it's not easy to deal with you through rude means. This second step is very crucial as most people give up after failing in the first attempt. You should have the tenacity to repeat your escalation and keep going higher and wider. Sometimes when escalation to a higher-up does not work, then you should use horizontal methods, innovative methods, indirect methods, and any other direction till you reach your goal.

Escalation is a double-edged sword and the same rules apply to you as well.

Finally, we can conclude this chapter with a great quote from Madonna who says, *'A lot of people are afraid to ask what they want. That's why they don't get what they want.'*

Dealing with Geeks

A computer dictionary defines geeks in many ways like, *'An individual who enjoys computers and technology, someone who is always immersed with computers, a computer expert or enthusiast, and so on.'* As a tech manager of any designation like CTO, CIO, etc., it's important to be able to effectively lead a team of geeks or IT support staff in your company. However, leading such geeks requires some special types of leadership skills that are different from the usual leadership fodder preached by traditional management consultants or books. So, what is that unique difference required in leading geeks? This chapter describes five important tips IT leaders must learn to lead geeks, whether they are within their own organizations or from outside.

Accept: Unless you are a megalomaniac you must acknowledge and accept that many of the techies you are supposed to lead are usually smarter and more talented than you. Also, many of the techies you lead, whether you like it or not, are themselves technical leaders irrespective of the title or salary they get. Hence, first switch off all intimidating components of a boss-subordinate behavior, however irresistible it is. They are turn-offs in relationships. For example, do not use popular irritating statements like, 'Don't come to me with problems, come to me with solutions,' or 'I know the solution, but I want to hear it from you,' or 'Show me the business value,' etc.

Knowledge: You can earn the respect of your team members only if you are able to converse with them in the language they use. That is, you must be able to talk and understand the technical stuff. You may be a good and kind person, but that is not enough to be a good technical manager or leader. If managers lack the required knowledge and advisory skills to coach, mentor, and supervise their department, they can agitate their team members to death. In addition to stressing their team members daily, managers will stress themselves more as they will be unable to lead effectively. This lack of knowledge can often lead to conflicts as you may make unrealistic demands on your techies, commit to impractical requests by customers, overload your techies, etc. Soon, it will become an ego conflict between the 'Knowledgeable and the Clueless.'

Constant learning: Understandably, a manager cannot be expected to have accurate knowledge from day one. To gain knowledge one must get into the deep water to understand the nitty-gritty of a new department's work, irrespective of their earlier experience. And no matter which department you manage, there will be some amount of new learning every day to keep abreast of the latest trends and happenings related to that particular industry. And you should be able to roll up your sleeves and pitch in if necessary.

Don't switch topics: Many managers have the habit of switching to some other topic just for the sake of disagreeing or proving a point. For example, if techies talk technical stuff, many managers switch the topic to finance like ROI, business justification, etc. Or if techies talk costs, then they drop a smarty like, 'Cost is not a concern when it comes to customer satisfaction,' to throw them off guard. In other words, they just disagree for the sake of disagreeing to introduce a different viewpoint. However, if you believe your angle is more important, then learn to steer the topic smoothly without expecting them to read your mind and tell things that you like to hear.

Written communication: This is an extremely important skill that all techies must learn. The palest ink is better than the most retentive memory. Learn to put everything in writing in clear, simple language. Instead of giving speeches, talking, or advising for an hour, just summarize what you want and how you want it in a concise email. Reduce formal talkative meetings to an absolute minimum. Instead, have quick informal meetings with your techies at their usual haunts like data centers, cabling rooms, server rooms, etc. That way you will get to know their ground realities, practical difficulties, limitations, workloads, etc., rather than have vague ideas of what they do by reading status reports.

Of course, there are heaps of other best practices that an IT manager must learn. However, the above five are a good beginning in case you are not practicing them already. Finally, we can summarize this chapter with a quote from Thomas Watson who said, *'A manager is an assistant to his men.'*

Stop Defining and Typecasting Yourself

Let us start this chapter with a joke and a couple of real-world examples.

A sixty-year-old person walked into an army headquarters to inquire if he could apply for a soldier's vacancy. The surprised sergeant bluntly said, 'You are sixty years old. How can you even think of applying for a soldier's job?' Pausing for a moment the old man then asked, 'Okay then, how about making me a general?'

Some years ago, there was a newspaper incident about a mother lifting a heavy car and saving her child who was pinned underneath.

And in 2008, there was a case of a woman attacking a leopard that was holding her child in the Katarnia Ghat Wildlife Sanctuary, Uttar Pradesh, India. The woman pounced on the leopard with some weapon she had and forced the big cat to release her child and run away.

The above examples can actually teach you a valuable lesson. And the lesson is that every human being is fundamentally capable of exhibiting various behaviors ranging from pure cowardice to extreme forms of bravery. Under normal circumstances, these ladies would have never pounced on a leopard or lifted a heavy car. But the fear of losing their kids gave them some temporary superhuman strength to tackle the situation. So, as you can see, every human behavior is relative, situational, and not exactly definable. Our behaviors are actually dependent on several factors and triggers. However, one of the biggest mistakes you can make to limit your capabilities is to mistakenly typecast yourself as an individual of a specific nature or behavior.

For example, you may define yourself as a calm person, a shy person, a tough person, and so on. Apart from your personal beliefs, there are also countless surveys and self-assessment tests that try to define what sort of a person you are based on the answers you give to various questions. And in most organizations, HR departments frequently try to classify employees into various categories like future leaders, trainers, top guns, mediocre, etc. Even astrology tries to define people based on the months or dates on which they were born or on some star signs and so on. But all these are only partially true, as you will shortly see.

While the classification of humans can happen due to various reasons, very often you blindly accept such conclusions as real and start believing in them. If an assessment survey, manager, or questionnaire concludes you do not have any leadership skills, you unconsciously (and foolishly) start believing it as absolute truth. But, unknown to yourself, such things can put a serious mental roadblock on you and make you develop an inferiority complex.

More importantly, they cause unnecessary stress, anxiety, and fear to be constantly active inside you. For example, if you believe yourself to be a timid person, you will always get scared of meeting tough people or tough situations and will never be able to handle them. But the reality is most people don't know that every human being is capable of releasing many hidden strengths and weaknesses should the situation demand.

A Buddhist teacher, Lama Zopa Rinpoche, preaches as follows – *'Leave the mind in its natural, undisturbed state. Don't follow thoughts of this is a problem, that is a problem. Without labeling difficulties as problems, leave your mind in its natural state. In this way, you will stop seeing miserable conditions as problems.'* Now slightly modify this great teaching and stop trying to define yourself as any specific type of person. Don't call yourself brave, tough, good, bad, timid, shy, coward, etc. Your actions are all situation or circumstance based. You can exhibit various behaviors depending on the circumstances or situations. History has been full of true stories of how ordinary people have done extraordinary things because they were pushed to the wall. Essentially, you are capable of moderation or extremes should the situation demand. That is the beauty and ferocity of human nature. Once you understand that you are capable of complete flexibility, you become truly resilient.

Tips for practicing this technique:

- Never try to define yourself in absolute terms. All your behaviors are relative and situational. Remember, you are capable of various drastic behaviors depending on the situation or if pushed to the wall.

Stop Defining and Typecasting Yourself

- Never underestimate yourself or anyone else. Do not be overwhelmed by the apparent superiority of an opponent. Remember how a small child, David, eliminated the giant Goliath.

- In order to eliminate the habit of defining yourself as a specific person, do not classify yourself as a specific type of person. Think of yourself as completely flexible, ranging from pure timidity to absolute violence should the situation demand. Essentially, such thinking can release you from the invisible shackles that limit your true capabilities.

Not trying to define yourself as a specific type of person can also help you in handling various degrees of responsibilities and difficult tasks. For example, if you define and believe yourself as a weak person, you will never be able to handle apparently tough people. But if you are completely flexible in the way you look at your strengths, it gives you the psychological power to handle any type of person and situation calmly. Such thinking can make tough situations less stressful.

Not defining yourself does not mean you get the right to act irrational or cranky. And it does not mean you can wear a clown suit for a business meeting. You still need to adhere to laws, decency, respect, proper communication, acceptable behavior, etc. It just means you develop an inner self-confidence that can give you the courage to rise above your fears, limitations, inadequacies, etc., if the need arises.

Finally, we can end this chapter with a quote from Theodore Roosevelt who said, *'Whenever you are asked if you can do a job, tell them, "Certainly, I can!" Then get busy and find out how to do it.'*

Get Accustomed to Monotonous Jobs

A dictionary defines monotonous as tediously repetitious or lacking in variety. Many years ago, I happened to see a very happy postal worker during a visit to a post office. He was probably in his mid-thirties and his job was to issue stamps. When I visited the post office recently, many years later, I saw the same person still in the job of issuing stamps, as happy as before. Seeing him happy made me very happy for some strange reason. Here is a man with a not very exciting job, yet happy as a free bird. Essentially, he chose to be happy despite doing a monotonous job.

Similar to the saying, 'Beauty is in the eyes of the beholder,' a job can be highly exciting or extremely boring depending on the doer. The enjoyment of a job depends on several factors like age, health, salary, education, opportunities, etc. Even supposedly exciting jobs cannot remain perpetually exciting or sustainable for years and years. For example, when you are young and a famous football player you may feel it's the best job in the world. But think again. Can you keep playing football for the next thirty or forty years? Obviously not. In all probability, you will end your playing career within a few years and end up having a desk job somewhere.

Many people dream that someday their humdrum lives will suddenly change for the better by suddenly becoming famous somehow, or winning a lottery, or some magic will happen like what happened to Cinderella. And they can live happily ever after as most fairy tales usually end. But unfortunately, such dreams come true for maybe one in ten million people. A lot of jobs on this planet are indeed monotonous and repetitive. Very few jobs exist that can be classified as perpetually exciting, interesting, and financially rewarding.

For example, the jobs of postal workers, traffic police, drivers, postmen, shop owners, security guards, civil servants, factory workers, laundry workers, salespeople, etc., are all monotonous. Even top executives and famous personalities with fancy incomes also feel tired and bored after some time, though they may not admit it openly. Either the work gets physically tiring, mentally stressful, or the joy is

Get Accustomed to Monotonous Jobs

slowly going away. Probably, even famous people like Donald Trump, Steven Spielberg, and Bill Gates may dread the Monday morning alarm and secretly feel, 'Oh, My God. Here comes a new week and another hundred million dollars to earn. How boring!!'

It's not always necessary for someone to criticize or harass you to feel bad about your job. If you believe you are in a boring or monotonous job, then you will soon tend to criticize yourself. You will start comparing your job with others who may have a great job. In economics, there is a law of diminishing returns, which states, 'The tendency for a continuing application of effort or skill toward a particular project or goal to decline in effectiveness after a certain level of result has been achieved.' Applied to jobs, the brain refuses to accept even exciting work as perpetually exciting. A point of saturation will be reached sooner or later where you will start criticizing your job silently.

I have seen software programmers and graphic designers who were extremely passionate about their jobs in their earlier years lose enthusiasm after a couple of years. Apparently, it's the same exciting work, a better salary, and a fancy title, but the joy is gone. Most jobs are not really monotonous, but the feeling of fun would have gone from the job. Even a top scientist, who has worked passionately and relentlessly to win a Nobel Prize, may rarely have the same passion a second time to attempt another Nobel Prize. So, there is no such thing as a perpetually exciting or a perpetually boring job. If you are willing to accept this, then life will be a lot easier to handle and you will also have less stress. And there are several ways to ensure that a monotonous job does not kill your zest in life.

Tips for practicing this technique

As children, everyone would have dreamt of becoming pilots, doctors, scientists, astronauts, and so on. But lack of proper education, poor opportunities, fate, and umpteen other reasons land people in various types of jobs totally unrelated to their dreams. Only a very small percentage of people get the jobs they really like to do for the rest of their lives.

It is important to accept the fact that most jobs do get monotonous after some time. But it need not make you miserable. Just imagine yourself without a job, with a bunch of unpaid bills and loan sharks pounding on your door. That can suddenly make you excited about your boring job.

Though there is nothing worse than a boring job, you can train yourself to be happy by accepting your limitations and trying to find some ways to break the monotony. If you start hating and disliking monotonous jobs, they can impact your health and peace of mind. And when you are tired and complain about your job, think of the unemployed, the needy, and those who wish they had your job.

Do not expect your managers or the organization to keep you constantly happy and motivated. It's not possible or sustainable. Look for other ways and means to keep yourself happy. For example, having a hobby can create that much-needed diversion from constantly brooding about your monotonous job.

Look around your home, town, or city, and you will see people doing jobs worse than yours. Occasionally, compare yourself with the downtrodden and homeless people who have more difficulties than you. There are even people out there who are awaiting the death penalty. Suddenly, you will realize your job and status in life are far superior to most others.

Never insult your job or the type of work. There is an interesting story about a poor cobbler who had a kit containing the tools required for his job. One day, he purchased a lottery ticket, noted the number on a piece of paper, and gave the ticket to his wife for safekeeping. Luckily, his number won the first prize, which was a huge sum of money. In his jubilation, he became arrogant and threw his toolkit into a wild river stating he had no use for the cursed thing henceforth. Rushing home, he asked for the ticket. His wife replied that she had kept the ticket inside the toolkit as she thought that would be the best place for safekeeping. So, the cobbler lost the tools required for his livelihood and also his potential fortune. What this story can teach you is the fact that all jobs are sacred in a way. The job you do may not be interesting or palatable, but never insult your job or the work you do.

Many people often change jobs when they start getting monotonous. Unless you are willing to switch careers, the next job in the same type of industry for your work experience will also become monotonous after the initial excitement. For example, a financial accountant may switch from company A to company

Get Accustomed to Monotonous Jobs

B, but the nature of the job is essentially the same. Perhaps a little more salary, a fancier job title, a better car, and a few other perks, but the job does get monotonous over time. Secondly, switching a career from one field to another is not easy for most people. For example, switching from software development to television advertising may not be achievable, unless you are willing to take risks and start fresh.

People often think they can survive with their passion or hobby. But a passion for something is not necessarily a viable and sound business option. And not every passion can generate a sustained income for years and years. Many people have strong passions for hobbies like creative arts, teaching, writing, or something they love to do. But before jumping ship just give it a hard thought as to whether those passions can bring you enough money to lead a decent life. The job you love to do may not necessarily feed you (and your dependents) on a sustained basis. Remember, feeling strongly about an idea is different from a profitable business. Don't do anything stupid like quitting your monotonous job without any alternate income and putting yourself or your family in trouble. So, learn to love your monotonous job for the paycheck and the security it brings. It's better to have a job that regularly brings in some money than follow a passion that may or may not shield you and your family from financial troubles. Remember, you owe your family a decent living and a paying job would pay your bills, provide health and life insurance, your kids' fees, and protect your family.

Finally, we can end this chapter with a great quote from Dean Koontz who said, *'Six billion of us walking the planet, six billion smaller worlds on the bigger one. Shoe salesmen and short-order cooks who look boring from the outside – some have weirder lives than you. Six billion stories, everyone an epic, full of tragedy and triumph, good and evil, despair and hope. You and me – we aren't so special, brother.'*

Other Books by the Author

Personal Planner

Personal Disaster Preparedness Planner
Organize your Information, Belongings, and Activities to Protect your Family in a Crisis

Humor Books

Become a Dictator
A Short and Snappy Guide

Become a Modern Artist
The Greatest and Easiest Job on Earth

Big Money
Top Secret Guide to the Stock Market Circus

The Mirage Peddlers
How to Become an Advertising Guru

The Mud Horse
Fantastic Jobs for Firebrand Feminists

Spirituality Books

The Miracle Law
The Pristine Path to Purpose and Prosperity

The Inventor of Nothing
A Mild and Wild Chat with the Brilliant Cosmic Designer

Personal Development Books

The Power of Laziness
Discovering the Wisdom of Slowness

The Extreme Minimalist
Discovering the Joys of Minimalism and Frugality

Get to the Point
A Short and Snappy Guide

The Curses of a Thousand Mothers
How We Pursue Joyful Sins

The Long Fuse
Why the Buddha Never Took Aspirin

No Easy Future!
Seven Habits to Tackle Tomorrow

Other Books by the Author

The Compass Mind
A Short Guide to Think in All Directions

Start Saying NO!
How to Stop Living for Others and Start Pursuing your Goals

The Gibraltar Briefcase
The Wise Weapons of Exceptional Executives

The Glass Prison
The How to Stay Productive during a Lockdown

Children Books

Secret Trip to a Jolly Jungle
The Adventures of Tommy and his Magic Spaceship

Secret Trip into the Ocean
The Adventures of Tommy and his Magic Spaceship

Secret Trip to a Treasure Island
The Adventures of Tommy and his Magic Spaceship

Secret Trip to Outer Space
The Adventures of Tommy and his Magic Spaceship

Other Books by the Author

The Magic Apple and his Mighty Friends

Technology Books

IT Asset Management
A Practical Guide for Technical and Business Executives

Disaster Recovery and Business Continuity
A Quick Guide for Organizations and Business Managers

Practical IT Service Management
A Concise Guide for Busy Executives

Fiction Books

FINK!
The Mafia's Nightmare

The Patriot's Confession
A Spy Thriller

The World's Shortest Novels
The Sixty Seconds Bookshelf

Personal Development Magazine
Wealth of the Wise

All the above books are available in both Paperback and eBook on all major book retailers

Author Services

Become an Author Course - Do you dream of becoming an Author? Do you want to share your Knowledge, Imagination, or Experience and write your first Fiction or Non-Fiction Book? Then take my Self-Paced Video Course on Thinkific for just US$79.95. The link is below.

https://thejendra.thinkific.com/courses/how-to-become-an-author-and-self-publish-your-book

Publish your Book Project - If you have already written a book and want to publish it, then I can help you to Self-Publish it Worldwide on Amazon, Apple, Kobo, BN, Google Play, Flipkart, and other book retailers in both Paperback and all eBook formats through my unique Assisted Self Publishing method.

Visit http://www.author-world.com for details

About the Author

Good day. My name is **Thejendra Sreenivas**. I was a Technology Manager in the IT industry for nearly 30 years. Before entering the IT industry, I was also an electronics lecturer for a short duration.

I have written and self-published 35+ books on various subjects. All my books are available in both Paperback and Kindle on Amazon and as an eBook on Apple, Kobo, B&N, Google Play, and many other retailers. I am also the Editor and Publisher of a font-optimized digital magazine called **Self Improvement International** which contains articles on personal development, workplace issues, humor, writing, and publishing.

I am now a **Book Publishing Coach** and offer services like *Assisted Self-Publishing, Manuscript Formatting, Facebook Ads, Ghostwriting, One Page Websites, Article Writing, and Podcast Creation*. In addition, I also offer Personal Development Coaching.

Please visit my web cave - **www.thejendra.com** or **www.author-world.com** for details of my books, magazine, and coaching information.

www.ingramcontent.com/pod-product-compliance
Lightning Source LLC
Chambersburg PA
CBHW021411210526

45463CB00001B/322